DEVON'S COASTLINE
AND COASTAL WATERS

Aspects of Man's
Relationship with the Sea

DEVON'S COASTLINE AND COASTAL WATERS

Aspects of Man's Relationship with the Sea

Edited by
David J Starkey

**Exeter Maritime Studies
No. 3**

EXETER MARITIME STUDIES

General Editor: Stephen Fisher

1. *Spanish Armada Prisoners. The Story of the Nuestra Señora del Rosario and her Crew and Other Prisoners in England 1587-97*, by Paula Martin (1988)

2. *Lisbon as a Port Town, the British Seaman and Other Maritime Themes*, edited by Stephen Fisher (1988)

3. *Devon's Coastline and Coastal Waters: Aspects of Man's Relationship with the Sea*, edited by David J. Starkey

4. *British Privateering Enterprise in the Eighteenth Century*, by David J. Starkey (forthcoming winter 1988-89)

Devon's Coastline and Coastal Waters:
Aspects of Man's Relationship with the Sea
First published 1988 by the
University of Exeter

© 1988 Department of Economic History
University of Exeter
ISBN 0 85989 314 6

Exeter University Publications
Reed Hall
Streatham Drive
Exeter, Devon
EX4 4QR

Typeset by TEX at the University of Exeter

Printed and Bound in Great Britain
by Short Run Press Ltd, Exeter

For
Little Frank

Acknowledgements

On behalf of the Steering Committee of the Maritime History of Devon Project, thanks are due to the staff of the University's Crossmead Conference Centre for providing such excellent accommodation for the symposium; to Celia Manning and Sue Murch for typing drafts of the papers; to Rodney Fry for drawing the figures; to Sue Milward for preparing the type-setting; and to Barbara Mennell and her staff for their ready help in the publication of this work.

CONTENTS

Frontispiece

The portion of the chart on the front cover is taken from John Thornton's *The English Pilot, The Third Book* published in London 1703. It is a copy of *A Large Chart of the Channel between England and France done from the Newest and Best Surveys* drawn by Joel Gascoyne in 1701. After five years in Cornwall, 1694-1699, surveying estates and producing his near one-inch-to-the mile map of the county, Joel Gascoyne returned to London where he renewed his association with his former master John Thornton. Both men had been Thames-side manuscript chart-makers linked in a master-apprentice relationship in the Drapers' Company. In the period c.1698-1708 John Thornton was one of the most competent and distinguished chart-makers in England. He gained and deserved this reputation for the way in which he promptly updated his charts as new material came to hand. Within a short time of Joel Gascoyne completing his pioneer map of Cornwall his new outline of its coast appeared on *A Large Chart of the Channel* referred to above; it has been described as 'one of the most important maps ever made' and 'the parent of a most numerous progeny'. It quickly became the standard chart for the English Channel. Alongside the new data with regard to magnetic variation and tides emanating from the pioneering work of the illustrious Edmond Halley undertaken in the closing years of the seventeenth century, the other significant new contribution was the much improved configuration and geographical location of Cornwall resulting from the work of Joel Gascoyne. This can be detected even in the version appearing here if the sophisticated outline for Cornwall is contrasted with the still crude depiction of the coastline of Devon.

Typical of the cartography of this period is the placing of vine-leaf enclosed map insets both in the sea and on the land. An enlarged inset of Plymouth Sound has been inserted into the centre of Devon and the beginning of another for the approaches to the Isle of Wight appears to its right.

It is ironic that John Thornton dedicated this chart to Sir Cloudisley Shovell who perished on the Isles of Scilly in 1707. Joel Gascoyne's surveying activities in the West Country did not include the Scillies. With hindsight, how unfortunate!

British chart-making evolved from the Mediterranean-derived Portolan Charts, the most characteristic feature of which was the network of radiating rhumb lines, focusing on a central intersection and with, normally, sixteen secondary intersections, each with its complement of radiating rhumbs. These intersections were frequently beautified by elaborate compass roses, one of which is reproduced on the back cover.

William Ravenhill

Cover design by Delphine Jones

INTRODUCTION

The papers collected in this volume were presented to the second symposium of the Maritime History of Devon Project held at the University of Exeter on 7-8 March 1987. Participating in this meeting were contributors to the Project, and others with an interest in the maritime dimension of Devon's historical experience. The broad nature of this subject – of 'maritime history' in general – is reflected in the range of expertise represented at the symposium; thus, archaeologists, cartographers, geologists, marine biologists and professional seafarers added their specialist knowledge to the more conventional wisdom of the political, social and economic historians. Indeed, it was with these diverse areas that the meeting was principally concerned, for the adoption of the broad theme of 'man's relationship with the sea' dictated that discussion should focus on the physical characteristics of the sea and coast, and man's attempts to come to terms with his natural environment.

In studying such factors, scholars frequently refer to the contradictory character of the sea. At once a barrier, a highway, a store of wealth, the sea has served to inhibit and to stimulate human economic activity. The age-old, and continuing, attempts to reconcile these contradictions – to create a highway out of the barrier, to exploit the riches of the deep without destroying them – have involved countless practical experiments and various forms of scientific enquiry. In this process man has acquired the knowledge and the experience to overcome many of the constraints, and to exploit many of the opportunities, presented to him by the sea. The application of various of these skills feature in each of the contributions to this volume. Thus, Professor Ravenhill charts the development of cartography from pre-Roman times to the nineteenth century, from the rudimentary memory of the coast's configuration which father passed on to son, to the relatively sophisticated attempts of chart-makers to locate accurately the latitude and longitude of key navigational points such as the Lizard and Start Point. Gradual improvements in the accuracy of these calculations made the navigation of coastal waters much safer for seafarers, though as late as the 1920s, as Edmund Eglinton's paper indicates, there was still no substitute for detailed first-hand experience in negotiating difficult waters. In this instance, it was the 'bushy stick', planted deliberately as an aid for navigation, that guided the *Mary Fletcher* into the Yeo River, and not the charts drawn by professional surveyors. Such an aid, in its own way, was therefore of some significance to the isolated communities between Clevedon and Weston – 'I never seed a place as dreary as this' – for which the *Mary Fletcher's* cargo of coal was bound.

If the treacherous currents and shifting banks of the Yeo represented a particular obstacle in the handling of coastal vessels, there were more general problems involved in handling the three-masted 'fully-rigged' sailing ship. The principles underlying the operation of these vessels, which carried the bulk of the world's trade until the late nineteenth century, are discussed by Peter Allington. Wind, tide and current are the raw materials which the sailing master has to harness, while the characteristics of his vessel – hull, lading, sail plan – further limit his options and test his skill. Such elements have to be understood and mastered if the sailing ship is to operate efficiently and safely, and thus 'shiphandling' is an important factor in the maritime economy, facilitating the carriage of goods and people. Naturally, these cargoes have to be loaded and discharged on land, though the point where this transfer is effected is subject to a number of variables. Alan Carr isolates one such factor, the tidal range, and considers its significance in determining the location of ports, the character of harbour installations, and the size of vessel a port might accommodate. This physical factor is related to man's economic requirements; thus, if the incentive exists, attempts to nullify the effects of an inopportune tidal range are undertaken, and substantial quantities of capital are invested in harbour works.

Man's relationship with the sea is seen in a rather different light in the remaining paper. While chart-making, shiphandling and port installations have developed in response to the problems and dangers associated with using the sea as a medium of transportation, the extraction of fish from its depths represents a more direct exploitation of the natural environment. For centuries this extractive industry has sustained a host of coastal communities in Devon and around the shores of Britain, yet its prosperity has depended ultimately upon the abundance, or otherwise, of the harvest. Many factors combine to condition this bounty of the sea, and the paper of Southward, Boalch and Maddock addresses one of the more important variables, climate, and assesses its long-term significance in determining the relative abundance of herring and pilchard off the south-west peninsula. In detecting a correlation between climatic fluctuations and changes in the population of these species, the authors help to explain the contrasting fortunes apparent in the herring and pilchard fisheries of Devon and Cornwall over the last 400 years. Here, at least, is one aspect of the natural environment that man has failed to influence in his favour, for over-fishing and pollution have been his principal contributions to date.

While the principal objective of the Maritime History of Devon Project is to further our understanding of Devon's maritime past, it is clear that this can only be achieved by placing the county's experience in a wider context, whether regional, national, or even international. This concern is fully reflected in the set of papers in this volume. Thus, the marine cartography of Devon is viewed in relation to the charting of the south-west peninsula in general, and the location of that vital landfall for mariners, the Lizard, in particular; the fluctuating abundance of herring and pilchard stocks is seen as a factor conditioning the fisheries of Cornwall as well as Devon; the economic

2

incentives governing the response to the tidal range in Devon are contrasted with those evident in South Wales; the general principles of shiphandling apply to Devon's seafarers and to seafarers the world over; moreover, the 'rule of thumb' techniques which guided the *Mary Fletcher* across the Bristol Channel and safely into the Yeo were adopted by generations of seafarers in the British coastal trade. It is hoped, therefore, that this collection, in addressing some of the environmental factors which have restricted or encouraged man's marine endeavours, will be of interest to those adopting a broader perspective as well as to those concerned primarily with Devon's maritime history.

David J Starkey

THE MARINE CARTOGRAPHY OF DEVON IN THE CONTEXT OF SOUTH-WEST ENGLAND

William Ravenhill

Whether it be land space or sea space, space is best expressed by space itself, reduced in scale of course, to make it manageable. To state that is one thing but there is 'Nothing so difficult as a beginning'.[1] Byron's phrase with regard to 'poesy' may, with equal force, be applied to the charting of Devon and the peninsula of south-west England. For it must be true that sailing directions, even if only given in the simplest of graphical forms and verbal terms, must have been continuously in use since sailing began, a body of lore handed on from master to mate, to apprentice, or to son. An early manifestation that the coastal waters of south-west England were being repeatedly navigated presented itself some thirty years ago when two Roman signal stations on the north coast of Devon were being excavated.[2] Old Burrow (SS 7880 4936) and Martinhoe (SS 6626 4933), both of first century date, were manned respectively between A.D. 48-54 and A.D. 55-70. Their location on the edge of a high-cliffed coastline with superb and extensive views over the sea to the west, the north, and the east indicates convincingly that they were placed there to watch the Bristol Channel. They did not function in isolation but rather in close co-operation with patrolling ships of the *Classis Britannica*[3] probably working out from their Claudian base of *Abonae*, Sea Mills (ST 5493 7576). The main role of the *Classis Britannica* was the rapid transportation of provisions, materials, and troops to the war zones, but in addition to this close-support activity, it also acted in other capacities, such as patrolling hostile shores and even carrying out coastal explorations as Tacitus in the *Agricola* makes apparent.[4]

By the middle of the first century A.D. the Roman fleet had rounded Land's End and was operating in what we now call the Bristol Channel, not by any means the easiest of waters to work, with its capricious winds and treacherous tides. Old Burrow and Martinhoe functioned in a tactical context during the invasion and conquest phase only, their occupation ceasing after the subjugation of South Wales so they did not become permanent sea marks. Nevertheless, the use of the Bristol Channel for maritime activities did not cease. Sea Mills continued to serve as the outlet for the important Mendip metal-producing region; more important, however, is the way it is thought that Gloucester emerged as the mercantile centre serving a western region remote from London with a bias towards trade with the Mediterranean and

Gaul. The extensive frontage of wharves built of timber and stone implies a measure of trade that must have been considerable in both substance and stability.[5] When to this is added the Roman taste for wine and oil what must be envisaged is the existence, over some four centuries, of supply ships making passages to and around the South West. These seafaring trade links pose some questions that scholars have not as yet addressed. What aids did the Romans have to navigate these western seaways? Were they relying on some kind of up-dated *Periplus*, or had their maritime information taken a spatial form in the mind only as a mental map? Or had the sea-going chart emerged, and if so, would it have resembled the Ptolemaic delineation of south-west England, a form that would, indeed, have been of considerable value. In recent years, as a result of Professor O.A.W. Dilke's work, scholars have begun to appreciate the sophisticated cartographic accomplishments of the Romans as far as land mapping is concerned.[6] Is there, comparatively, a marine cartography yet to be unveiled? The pragmatic and economic needs of Empire predisposes one to assume there must have been. A contrary *argumentum ex silentio*, based on the non- survival of archive, does not tally with the intricate trade links and space relationships the Romans successfully established.

For the post-Roman period one is even less well informed about maritime activities but that they survived the withdrawal of the legions there can now be no doubt. One of the most revealing results of recent ceramic research in archaeology has been the demonstration that wheel-made pottery found on sites in Devon, Cornwall and Scilly, dating from the fifth to eighth centuries A.D., was imported from as far away as North Africa and the eastern Mediterranean.[7] What return cargoes there might have been to make the long-distance venture profitable can only be guessed, but there is no such doubt that vessels trading out of the Levant, Carthage and other famous Mediterranean ports of antiquity made the sea journey via the Straits of Gibraltar to our shores.[8] That these sailors navigated in the same way as the Romans and shared a similar knowledge of the sea routes there can be little doubt. One of the principal regular commodities traded, as expressed by the ceramic series, was wine, some of which clearly found its way to the religious communities of western Britain. There is considerable evidence of thalassic links continuing across the western seaways in the so-called Age of the Saints.[9] Their feats of seamanship emerge indirectly in the *Lives of the Celtic Saints* where it is frequently difficult to distinguish fact from fiction. The individuals concerned were literate, they were heirs to much in the Roman tradition, but whether they were graphicate is not known. Certain it is that many of the Celtic saints travelled extensively by sea using the coves and inlets of Devon and Cornwall, and for navigation must have relied on more than the guidance systems of a Divine Being.

The Mediterranean Sea was as much the highway of the medieval world as it had been for the classical peoples who developed their civilisations on its shores. The ancient *periplus* gradually evolved into the medieval Portolan; the portrayal of maritime space, so it would appear, like terrestrial space, reverted to the more cumbersome medium of written words. Just like the long, confusing lists of abuttals in manorial extents and terriers, at sea when what was held in the memory was given a physical form, it was by means of a small pocket book in which were listed the distances and later, as the use of the magnetic compass developed, the bearings of courses between capes, headlands, harbours, and some sea crossings. In time these written instructions were accompanied by drawings of coastlines; in the next stage the graphical element took precedence over the written, resulting gradually in the emergence of the sea-chart. At first the Italian cartographers called these *Chartae* or *Tabulae* but in the later Middle Ages, confusingly but logically, they became known as *portolani* since they were in reality written sailing directions rendered in spatial form. The term has survived into modern times, the distinction between the written and graphical forms being made by the addition portolan chart.

A comparable evolution occurred in the sea-faring of northern waters. What became known as *portolano* in the Mediterranean were called *roteiro* by the Portuguese, *routier* by the French, and rutter by the English. The earliest surviving rutter provides sailing directions for the circumnavigation of England and for a voyage to the Straits of Gibraltar. In its extant state it is a copy made in the reign of Edward IV, but it is based on older material and has been attributed to the year 1408. The detail for the South West when placed in context, reveals how by repetition of similar directional phrases these written directions can become confusing and cumbersome.

In the fairway between the Start and Lizard the course is east and west. And beware the hidden stones. All the havens be full at a west south west moon between Start and Lizard, the Land's End and Lizard lieth east south east and west north west.[10]

Furthermore, the information is limited, no distances are given, only compass courses, but even these, when interpreted spatially, leave much to be desired. The true bearing of Start to Lizard is 254°. The variation in the fifteenth century was to the east and so the compass bearing, if this is what the rutter is providing, will be obtained by subtracting from 254° making it smaller. When compared with the rutter's value of 270° the course suggested could be out by some 20° to 30°. The rutter is, however, not alone in presenting this false image of an east to west orientation for south-west England, as contemporary land-maps do likewise.

The lack of surviving examples before the end of the thirteenth century makes it difficult to be precise about the actual origin and early evolution of the portolan chart in the Mediterranean. For areas outside that sea there is less uncertainty, for whereas the delineation of the Mediterranean coastlines on the earliest portolan charts is relatively good, the Atlantic coasts by contrast are portrayed much less well, thus indicating that they had not long since been included. Similarly, the representation of the British coastline can be followed through from an early partial and inaccurate form, through several stages of improvement and extension, until a fuller coverage emerges.[11] The earliest known chart, the so-called *Carte Pisane*[12] of c.1275, so stylized as to suggest that it must have had predecessors, shows the Mediterranean with considerable sophistication, but outside the Pillars of Hercules, Iberia's Atlantic coast and Brittany are scarcely articulated. Britain is not recognisable, in truth far inferior to its delineation on Ptolemy's map. Even so, the only coast with annotations is the south coast with two of the six place-names assigned to the south-west pensinsula; this indicates how little British geography was known to the marine cartographers of the Mediterranean at this time. This poor state of delineation was to change quite quickly and effectively within a generation when organised Italian trade involved regular sailings to England, Ireland and Flanders. Great Britain appears as a recognisable form for the first time on a portolan chart about 1313; the south coast is depicted in some detail but the west coast is still not known and there is not as yet a north coast to Cornwall and Devon, and no Bristol Channel. These features were included on a chart made about 1327.

The Mediterranean-produced portolan charts continued in production for close on 300 years. In this period the British Isles were becoming more completely shown but as far as the South West was concerned there was not all that much improvement except in a small number of details. Indeed, Britain never approached either the accuracy or the completeness that characterized the Mediterranean area. Nevertheless, portolan chart-making initiated a tradition, and established a pattern as those which have survived exhibit a remarkable family likeness. Usually they are drawn on single skins of parchment which, beside retaining their natural shape, range in length from 3 to 5 feet and from 18 to 30 inches in depth. A number of conventions became almost sacrosanct; coastlines were drawn in black ink, coastal place-names and coastal features were inscribed inland and perpendicular to the coast. Most of these names were rendered in black but important harbours were in red, while national allegiances were indicated by means of coloured flags and banners. On occasions portolan charts have been called 'compass charts' encapsulating, as it were, the concept of the compass set down on a plane chart. To emphasize this aspect a master compass rose was drawn near to the centre with additional roses placed elsewhere. The lines indicating the points of the compass were extended outwards from the roses forming a schema of intersecting bearings; this pattern of intersecting lines, evolved when sailing ships could not be expected to steer closer than a quarter point, became the most characteristic feature of the portolan charts.

Alongside the compass, the portolan chart was the next most important of the navigational advantages possessed by the Mediterranean seamen of the fifteenth century. Nevertheless, it needs to be remembered that the charts were not without their shortcomings. No account was taken of the sphericity of the earth, the area being treated as a plane surface and without any indication of longitude and latitude. The bearings on which they were constructed were magnetic and orientation therefore differed from true geographical orientation by the variation. This can be detected in the way the magnetic north on the portolans is indicated by a number of parallel verticals, the convergence of meridians being ignored. The inevitable result is that straight lines drawn on the charts were only approximations to true rhumb lines. Moreover, the

8

variation changed markedly over the sea areas now being mapped but it did so over the length of the Mediterranean and so even there the charts are internally inconsistent. The fact that the variation changed from year to year at a different rate from place to place was a complication ignored on the charts. In spite of these deficiencies the portolans changed little in outline, style, or construction between the thirteenth and fifteenth centuries. The Mediterranean navigators, for whom in the main they were made, could get away with it since the range of latitude in which they operated was relatively small, the convergence of the meridians slight, and the discrepancy between bearing and rhumb not as worrying as errors arising from currents, winds and human frailty. In many respects, at this period, navigation was an art of approximation.

In the late fourteenth century the Italian, Spanish, and Catalan superiority in the production of charts was challenged by the Portuguese. France attracted Portuguese pilots and chart-makers into its service which in time led to the emergence of French chart-making activity in Normandy, and in particular, at Dieppe. Jean Rotz was of this school who, with others, came in due course into the service of Henry VIII.[13] The evolution of a north-west European chart-making industry in the hands of the French, the English, and particularly the Dutch was not long delayed. A survivor from these days is the map of the sea space between Land's End and the Exe estuary, drawn during Henry VIII's reign by a hand unknown.[14] The four sections, when butted, measure some 10 feet by 2 feet and could hardly have been of practical use on board a ship. Notwithstanding, it does possess some hydrographic information; it gives the distances between prominent headlands like the Lizard, Dodman, and Rame Head, and, incidentally, delineates the Lizard peninsula more correctly in shape than it was destined to be until 1699. Of interest too, in terms of a subsequent context, is the way in which estuaries are emphasised at the expense of the intervening coastal headlands. One wonders, however, whether by the nature of its making on four sheets intended to be butted, whether it did not help to nurture and perpetuate the false image of an east-west orientation for south-west England.

As the 'Discovery of the Sea'[15] began to exercise more persistently the minds of northern Europeans, one feature of coastal configuration which has already been hinted at, became immensely important. On the whole global surface of land and sea it falls to the lot of some few localities to emerge through time to become of outstanding significance; for example, the Straits of Gibraltar, the Bosphorous, the Straits of Hormuz. In our context it was the English Channel and the landfalls for entering it – the highway, the fairway, to all the countries of northern Europe. Northern seamen in the fifteenth century lagged behind their Mediterranean contemporaries in their methods of navigation, but in some aspects of coastal, as distinct from ocean navigation, they were, and needed to be, more expert. Even in their rutters certain aspects were made more explicit than in the *portolani*. This was especially true in dealing with tides, tidal streams, and the nature of the sea-bed. This reliance on soundings reflects the different nature of the English Channel from the

Mediterranean, where, for the most part, the land plunges down abruptly to give deep water close on shore. By contrast, on entry to the English Channel the sea-bed rises to the continental shelf by a clearly defined isoline at 100 fathoms.

With the great surge forward in maritime interests in the sixteenth century, mercantile activity, as a whole, was on a different scale and in a new dimension. To sea-going was added very much more ocean-going. For this, the simple port to port empiricism of the portolan chart was completely inadequate. It was beyond the skills of the fifteenth- and early sixteenth-century chart-makers to reconcile the requirements of dead-reckoning navigation with those of celestial navigation using a geographical or true orientation. The re-discovery of Ptolemy's *Geographia* by the western world after 1406 was as vital an incident for sailors as it was for the cosmographers and cartographers. Ocean-going required sailing in relation to the Ptolemaic global co-ordinate system of longitude and latitude. To determine one's longitude shipboard was beyond contemporary skills and so reliance was placed on 'finding and running down the latitude'. This involved steering a course which would bring a ship on to the latitude of the intended destination but well to seaward. Thereafter, by steering due east or due west it was hoped the intended landfall 'hove over the horizon'. As this new method of navigation was more widely adopted sailing manuals were printed with lengthening lists of key latitudes. In this new expanded space-relationship of ocean-sailing the largest number of voyages involved leaving and returning to the English Channel. It was absolutely vital, therefore, to get this key latitude for the entry correct. William Bourne, writing in 1577, articulated the spatial setting thus:

> Because it is necessary to be had in memory, because that it is a dangerous place to hit or fall with, to enter into the sleeve, [the Channel – La Manche] coming homewards out of Spain or Portugal, or from Barbaria, or any place from the southwards. A ship that cometh from any such place to seek the Isle of Ushant or the Lizard...

Bourne demonstrated further the key latitude technique:

> Thus much have I said for the entrance of the sleeve, to come to the river of Thames, and in the entrance in the midway between Ushant and the Lizard the pole Articke is elevated 50 degrees and a half.[16]

Owing to the hazards in the vicinity of Ushant and the dangerous north coast of Brittany and Normandy, the Lizard as landfall became of paramount importance. Modern latitude determinations of the Lizard, 49°57'32", and Ushant, 48°28'00", give a midway value of 49°17'46".

If Bourne's determinations were relied upon while 'running down the latitude', the ships' pilots would at best find themselves in the Bristol Channel instead of the English Channel; at worst, shipwrecked on the granite teeth of the Penwith peninsula or the north coast of Cornwall.

Hydrography and cartography should be inseparable twins, but they have not always been. In Elizabethan times the good father to such twins was

John Dee – the intellectual giant of the age, the Ptolemy of the Elizabethan period. In his *General and Rare Memorials pertayning to the Perfecte Arte of Navigation*, published in 1577, he indicated clearly and pointedly how Dutch marine surveying and charting was in advance of the British even in our own waters.

> And, of these sort of people they be, which (other whiles) by colours and pretence of coming about their feat of fishing, do subtly and secretly use soundings, and searching, of our channels, deeps, shoals, banks or bars, along the sea coasts, and in our haven mouths also, and up in our creeks, sometimes in our bays, and sometimes in our roads, &c. Taking good marks, for avoiding of the dangers: And also trying good landings. And (so, making perfect charts of all our coasts, round about England and Ireland)...[17]

What John Dee was deploring, however, led to an outstanding achievement in nautical cartographic synthesis by the Dutch in the late sixteenth century. Lucas Janszoon Waghenaer codified and presented the then current nautical knowledge of western Europe in his *De Spieghel der Zeevaerdt*,[18] printed in Leiden in 1584-5. It was a major advance in the evolution of hydrographic publication. Within the covers of one volume the seaman was provided with a manual of practical navigation, a set of *printed* charts drawn to a common scale, sailing directions, and numerous tables. The charts were on a scale large enough for pilotage with offshore detail of vital consequence to the mariners, such as soundings, shallows, sea-marks, anchorages and channels. On shore he provided coastal views, vertically projected as seen from the sea. His charts were clearly intended for pilotage, not navigation so much, because there is deliberate distortion of the coastline by the enlargement of the entrances to rivers and havens, a feature already encountered. Drawings of ships served a dual function; they were decorative and were also useful since they depicted the type of vessel met with off various stretches of coast. This facilitated position finding. The English Lord High Admiral was so impressed with *De Spieghel* he laid it before the Privy Council for authorization to translate it and publish it in England. When it appeared in 1588 with the title *The Mariners Mirrovr*,[19] a significant difference between the Dutch and English versions was the treatment of the sea surfaces; in the latter they were left blank deliberately, so as to facilitate additions and amendments to the information – a ploy clearly expressive of the enquiring and scientifically-oriented spirit of the times.

John Dee was also involved in the highly innovative national mapping undertaken by Christopher Saxton in the years 1574-83. He produced two masterpieces, the so-called 'Atlas of county maps', and, more significantly for the present context, the large general map published in 1583, wherein Britain, by a most sophisticated treatment of the geographical co-ordinates, has been placed in its global context by means of the Donis projection.[20] While Saxton must be praised for his overall accuracy he seriously misaligned the most important part of the country as far as contemporary marine navigation was concerned: the peninsula of south-west England appears again with an orientation too pointedly in an east to west direction.[21] Saxton's delineation of the British coastline overall was far superior to that of any previous mapmaker but, surprisingly, chart-makers for a long time to come ignored his excellence and continued to depict the country crudely. Cross fertilization between cartography and hydrography seemed for a time to be lacking, a loss being deplored as late as 1717; thus,

> Tis observable, that not only the sea coasts, in two several maps of the same parts commonly differ strangely from each other, but also rarely ever any agree in that respect with the sea charts which happens for want of consulting the Wagonners, either through their little concern for exactness, or imagining a map is to be drawn only by a map, and a chart from a chart.[22]

The merit of printed charts was that they tended to eliminate copying errors and to standardize hydrographical information. In Britain, however, it was the manuscript chart-makers who flourished particularly with regard to ocean-going charts. A noteworthy early example was produced by Thomas Hood in 1596. It merits notice since it is one of the earliest, possibly the earliest, to show soundings out to sea as far as the 100 fathom line and to have a latitude scale.[23] These two items of hydrographical information could be combined to good effect, particularly on approaching the entrance to the English Channel. A ship's navigator, having taken the altitude of the sun at noon or the pole star at dusk, to obtain the required key latitude and then 'running down this latitude' could subsequently take deep soundings until the sea-bed was encountered at the 100 fathom line. A position line for the latitude of entry could then be intersected with a position line for the sounding, thus providing a fix, though the sixteenth-century seaman would not have been familiar with our modern terminology.

Hood's chart was a manuscript plane chart but almost contemporaneously, that is in 1599, Edward Wright had constructed his table of Meridional Parts by a continuous summation of secants and produced a chart of roughly the same area on a Mercator's Projection.[24] Wright's chart was printed and included another important feature, namely information about magnetic variation. Such innovations express, at least in some quarters, the application of scientific and mathematical principles to navigation which, during the reign of Elizabeth, brought England abreast, and in some respects ahead, of her continental rivals in marine cartography. Alongside this innovative, imaginative, and intellectual thrust there was, of course, conservatism and suspicion of new-fangled techniques and instruments. William Bourne could justifiably grumble about 'ancient masters of ships' who 'derided and mocked them that have occupied their cards and plats ... saying: that they cared not for their sheeps skins'. Even these 'sheeps skins', still for the most part plane charts, had now been superseded by Edward Wright's Mercator-chart sailing. Many seamen were, however, unable to make use of these new advances and loathe to give up old practices and well-tried procedures even though they were known to be inefficient and hazardous. There was something to be said for their point of view. The charts, though of considerable use, could not claim to be accurate and reliable. They needed to be used with extreme caution. After all, how many of them could possibly have been based on good surveys and for how many places on the surface of the whole globe had geographical co-ordinates been determined to a high order of accuracy. It was a century before Mercator charts and Mercator sailing replaced the plane charts and, as far as Britain was concerned, before printed charts replaced the manuscript 'sheeps skins'.[25]

A school of manuscript chart-makers in the portolan tradition and mould emerged and flourished throughout the seventeenth century in England. They plied their trade in shops lining the streets and alleys that led down to the waterfront on the north bank of the Thames down river from the Tower of London. These chart-makers were linked in a master-apprentice relationship in the Drapers' Company.[26] One of their number, Joel Gascoyne, 1650-1705, features prominently not only in a national but also in a regional context.[27] In the 1670s the English cartographer John Seller tried to break the Dutch monopoly of publishing atlases of printed maps. Samuel Pepys as Secretary to the Navy, consulted Joel Gascoyne in October 1680 on the accuracy and quality of Seller's products as compared with those of the Dutch.[28] From what happened shortly afterwards Gascoyne's report must have been very damning. Although printed in England some of Seller's charts were pulled off old Dutch copper plates, touched up in places, to give them the appearance of being new. The sequel to this was that after nearly one hundred years of reliance on printed Dutch charts, Pepys issued an Admiralty Order, in June 1681, assigning a naval officer, Captain Greenvile Collins, to the task of surveying the coasts and harbours. A significant practical advance was made on 23 June 1681 when Charles II issued a proclamation announcing the appointment of Collins to the command of the yacht *Merlin*

> to make a survey of the sea coasts of the kingdom by measuring all
> the sea coasts with a chain and taking all the bearings of all the
> headlands with their exact latitudes... [29]

The work of survey took place between 1681 and 1688, and culminated in 1693 with the publication of *Great Britain's Coasting Pilot*.[30] One would have expected the outcome of this government-sponsored survey to have been published by a government agency but this was not the case and the work was left to a private printer. It was the first systematic survey of Britain's coastal waters and the first marine atlas printed in London from original surveys. Some of the charts first became available in the early 1680s and almost immediately they began to receive critical comment, not least by some of the Fellows of the Royal Society. This is not surprising; if one examines the chart for the Lizard, the important contemporary landfall, the peninsula is crudely delineated and the latitude determination of 50° is too far north by 2'28". Technically, the surveying principles Collins applied were right, but the methods he employed left much to be desired, and the support he received was woefully inadequate. Marine surveying should be based on a previously conducted land survey of the coastline but to do so by open traverses with chain and compass with little or no overall control will inevitably give rise to cumulative errors. Doubt has even been expressed as to whether he actually used this method everywhere and not the older running surveys of sailed traverses. Furthermore, the whole work was completed in a remarkably short period of time; for instance, he had surveyed the Channel from Dover to Land's End by 1682! For such an intricate and complex undertaking this is incredibly swift progress, especially when the meagre resources in terms of manpower and facilities are taken into account. At the time, those who commissioned the work, must have had but little conception of the magnitude of the task. Later they did. 'And then', Pepys reflected, 'it is meet to consider how far a single man is to be trusted alone on a business of this weight and nature'.[31] Nevertheless, after the first edition of 1693, some 12 editions were to follow, the volume being left on the market with remarkably little change until 1792 by which time the charts must have been hopelessly out of date.

Just before the first edition of the *Coasting Pilot* appeared in 1693, Joel Gascoyne ceased to be a member of the Drapers' Company,[32] gave up his business as a manuscript chart-maker and for the rest of his life devoted himself almost exclusively to landsurveying, an occupation at which he became a much sought-after practitioner. From commissions around London by some of the distinguished in the capital, he was wooed to south-west England by the Robartes and the Grenville families; the outcome after some years being a large number of estate surveys and these in turn culminating in the first near one-inch-to-the-mile map of any British county, that is Cornwall. For the first time also the Cornish coastline and with it the Lizard was mapped to a very high relative standard.[33] 'As to its position with respect to the heavens', declared Herman Moll in 1724,

> many accurate observations of later years have been made. Mr Gas-
> coigne, who surveyed Cornwall and is a gentleman of distinguished
> ability, in the art of surveying has justly fixed the Lizard Point...[34]

How 'justly' in a relative sense can be estimated from the ordinates in Figure 1 but in actual terms he fixed the Lizard 1'34" south of its modern determination, the south error being the safer one for mariners. However, for nearly half a century after 1699, the value of 49°55' assigned by the illustrious Edmond Halley (1656-1742), held sway.

Halley's value was, however, not considered so sacrosanct as not to be worth checking when, in 1740, Parliament passed 'An Act for Surveying the Chief ports and headlands on the Coasts of Great Britain ... in order to the more exact determinations of the longitude and latitude thereof'.[35] For this task £500 was given to the irrepressible William Whiston (1667-1752), the expelled Lucasian Professor of Natural Philosophy at Cambridge. Earlier, in 1714, he had been involved with Sir Isaac Newton in the lobbying which brought into being the Board of Longitude, a body specifically created to attempt to solve the problem of ascertaining longitude at sea. Whiston argued convincingly that it would be of little value to a navigator to be able to find longitude at sea if his landfall was at fault, and the grant was accordingly

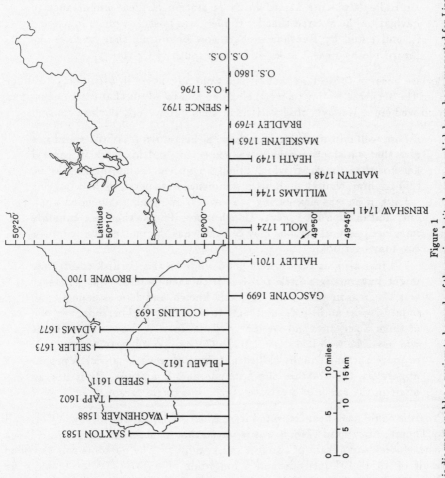

Figure 1

This diagram enables a review to be made of the various latitude values which have been suggested for Lizard Point. They are arranged chronologically in the form of ordinates drawn to scale reading from left to right.

15

made to him in 1740 for this latter purpose. Not surprisingly, Lizard Point came in for almost immediate attention, and Whiston sent J. Renshaw to observe there in 1741. His visit was subsequently recalled in a letter written by William Borlase, FRS, DCL, Rector of Ludgvan and Vicar of St Just in Cornwall. Renshaw and another person arrived at Lizard with

> a well appointed apparatus, the best I have ever seen, of all travelling instruments for observation. Upon talking with Renshaw concerning Dr Halley's placing Lizard Point (a station of great importance in navigation) he averred that Dr H[alle]y was mistaken much in placing it; and I find by Renshaw's chart now before me that he fixes the Lizard p[oin]t near 7 miles and a half south of Dr Halley.

Borlase goes on to declare that 'it is a bold adventure in astronomy to differ from the accurate Halley'; nevertheless, he had to admit that instruments had improved since Halley's observations in 1699. 'However', Borlase continues,

> if I am well informed, Mr R[enshaw] at his return to Whiston did not give that satisfaction which was expected, and his work in general has not that character which might be wished. Some things may be said for him, that though his instruments were good, he had but one second, if he was sick during the voyage, everything depended upon one, and in such nice points (much more difficult than is commonly imagined) several persons may correct what the inattention of one or two may overlook.
>
> I fear also, as they were a good while on the Cornish coast, they might have made a little too free with their bottle – but whatever was the reason their chart is little known and less esteemed, and indeed it was an ill-judged scheme to send only two persons, and one of them a servant, and we may depend upon it that our headlands will never be well laid down till the Government directs at least four or more persons equally skilled in taking observations with a proper apparatus, to ascertain the Latitude and Longitude. It is not an affair in the reach of a private purse, or a single person.[36]

Progress could have been expected from a new, independent survey of Cornwall by Thomas Martyn in 1748; it was reported that he observed from Lizard Point 'with Hadley's quadrant of two feet radius only'.[37] The outcome was the poor result of 49°48'49" latitude and a longitude of 05°37'39"W of London, as Figure 2 shows. It was the co-ordinate values on this map and others which were in the mind of William Borlase when he penned the letter referred to above, as well as an earlier one in the same year (1756), in similar terms, to the newly founded Society for the Encouragement of Arts, Manufactures and Commerce of London;[38] thus,

> the headlands of all our shores are at this time disputed; and even where Halley himself made his observations. You can't imagine what differences in the longitudes, latitudes distances and projections of

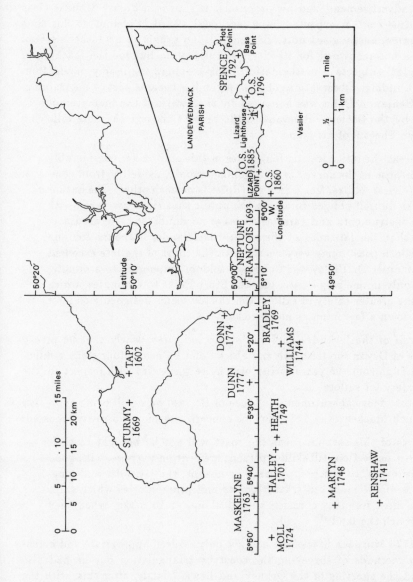

Figure 2

Early determinations of the latitude and longitude of Lizard Point
plotted in relation to recently calculated values

17

promontories and towns have occurred in the examination of author's charts and maps of this little county.[39]

In 1759 the Society offered a 'Premium' for Surveys of Counties with quite specific requirements. Benjamin Donn of Bideford responded to the Society's advertisement, and his proposals, as shown in Figure 3, make clear the maritime content expected for a successful award. Bideford at this time was an active, bustling sea-port. Benjamin Donn taught in his father's school there; one not renowned for its classical curriculum but for the teaching of 'new-fangled' subjects – mathematics, book-keeping, astronomy, navigation, and ship building. Observations of celestial bodies became part of the training. In 1765 Benjamin Donn was honoured by the award of the first premium to be given by the Society. Relevant to the present context the note following appears on Sheet 9 of his map:

> Whereas the latitudes and longitudes in this map, differ considerably from those in the survey of an adjoining county, as well as from common charts, books, &c. which also differ from each other. The author thinks himself obliged to assure the public that these are taken with such instruments and care, as to leave no doubt of their accuracy; and that the latitudes of the points, headlands, harbours &c. on the south coast agree very nearly with the chart of the late excellent astronomer Dr Halley, the difference seldom amounting to a minute, and only in one single case, viz. the Start Point to 4 minutes, which for the greater safety of sailors, the Doctor seems designedly to have laid down a few minutes more south.

An analysis of the latitudes on Donn's map indicates clearly that he placed the whole of Devon too far north and Start Point by nearly four statute miles. Halley, though some 65 years earlier, was more successful with respect to 'the greater safety for sailors'.

Almost identical sentiments to those of Borlase were still being expressed by Murdoch Mackenzie in 1774, but his concern was more narrowly focussed:

> Charts of this sort i.e. near the coast will not be brought to their utmost perfection, till skillful persons are sent on purpose, with good instruments, to observe, on land, or near it, the latitudes and longitudes of the most remarkable points and promontories which ships have most frequent occasion to sail along, or to make, when they approach the land.[40]

By 1774 Murdoch Mackenzie had not only evolved appropriate and much-improved methods of surveying the coast by triangulation but he had also completed the charting of the Orkney and Lewis Islands; after this, with the support of the Admiralty, he surveyed the whole of the Irish coasts and the west coast of Britain as far as Carmarthen Bay. When he retired as Maritime Surveyor at the Admiralty, his place was taken, in 1771, by his nephew, Lieutenant Murdoch Mackenzie, junior. Two years later, before being assigned to other port and estuary surveys in eastern and southern England, he produced

PROPOSALS

For SURVEYING and MAKING

A NEW and ACCURATE MAP

OF

The County of Devon.

By *BENJAMIN DONN*,

Author of * The MATHEMATICAL ESSAYS.

CONDITIONS.

1. AS the Accuracy, and consequently the Value, of a Map must chiefly depend on the correctness of the Position, and horizontal Distances of the principal Places, particular Care will be taken to determine these in a new and rational Method, by the Assistance of a curious Set of Instruments, Trigonometrical Calculations, and Astronomical Observations.

2. Not only the Situation of the principal Towns, but also the Villages, Hamlets, Gentlemens Seats, Buildings of Antiquity, or Places esteemed on Account of any thing very curious either in Art or Nature, will be shewn, and distinguished: The Roads, Rivers, &c. described.

3. The Roads, (at least the High Roads) will be actually measured; and the Courses and Bearings of all the principal Rivers, together with the Plans of the Market Towns, &c. carefully taken, either by himself, or by Assistants properly qualified, for the greater Dispatch.

4. As the Tables of Latitudes and Longitudes, &c. in most Books of Navigation are very inaccurate, and still worse in Books of Geography (as is well known to the ingenious Masters of Ships), though the Safety of Ships, and consequently the Lives of Sailors, in a great Measure depends on the Accuracy of such Tables; it must be of the greatest Use to a Maritime County, to have its Sea Coasts accurately laid down, together with the Latitudes and Longitudes of the principal Harbours, Capes, or Headlands, with the Variation of the Compass, justly determined. Particular Care will therefore be taken to render this Part of the Survey as accurate as the Nature of such an Undertaking will permit. In a Word, the whole will be executed on a Plan approved of by the *Society for Encouragement of Arts, Manufactures, and Commerce.*

5. The Copper Plates shall be engraved by good Hands.

6. The Map will be about Six Feet in Length, and a proportionable Breadth; the Price of which to Subscribers is One Guinea & half in Sheets; or pasted on Canvas with Rollers Two Guineas; the Money to be paid on Delivery of the Map. It being manifest that the Execution of this Plan (which is already begun) will be attended with great Labour and Expence, it is hoped it will be encouraged by a handsome and speedy Subscription, that so necessary and useful an Undertaking may not be laid aside.

As the Author, for the greater Dispatch, intends to employ several Assistants, &c. which will greatly increase the Expence, he has been advised to fix a higher Price than was at first intended.

Subscriptions are taken in by the Author at *Bideford*, or in his Progress through the County: Also by Messrs. *Score*, *Thorn*, *Tozer*, and *Grigg*, Booksellers, Mr. *Coffin*, Engraver and Mapseller, and at *Moll's Coffee-house*, in *Exeter*; Mr. *Parkhouse* in *Tiverton*; Mr. *Haydon* at *Plymouth*; Mr. *Colley* at *Barnstaple*; and by almost all other Booksellers in the County; Also by Mr. *Manning* in *Launceston*, Mr. *Palmer* in *Bristol*, Mr. *Fletcher* in *Oxford*; Messrs. *Davey* and *Law* in *Ave-Mary-Lane*, Mr. *J. Bockland* in *Paternoster-Row*, Mr. *George Adams*, Instrument-Maker to His Royal Highness the Prince of *Wales*, in *Fleet-street*, *London*; Mr. *Frederic* at *Bath*; and Mr. *Goadby* in *Sherborne.*

* Being Essays on Vulgar and Decimal Arithmetick, &c. or The First Volume of a new Course of Mathematical Learning, which is recommended in The MONTHLY REVIEW for *July* 1758, to all who would study Arithmetick in a rational and scientific Manner: And the Critical Reviewers allow it to have many Advantages above any other Treatise on these Subjects, both in the Justness of the Method, and Accuracy of the Solutions.

Printed by ANDREW BRICE, in *Northgate-street, Exon.*

Figure 3
Benjamin Donn's Proposals
Note the maritime emphasis in paragraphs one and four

a manuscript chart of south-west Cornwall which just included the Lizard, but without any graduations.[41]

Considerable progress was, however, being made in this respect under the leadership of Nevil Maskelyne who was appointed the fifth Astronomer Royal in 1765. Two years previously he had published *The British Mariner's Guide* and provided for Lizard a value of 49°47'N for the latitude and 05°43'W longitude. This *Guide* may be considered the forerunner of the *Nautical Almanac*, which first appeared in 1766. In a Preface to the edition of 1769, Maskelyne dealt at length with the Lizard.[42] He claimed that the co-ordinates had never been determined by astronomical observations and therefore still remained uncertain. For *The British Mariner's Guide* he had deduced a longitude by comparing the position of the Lizard with that of Liskeard 'by the help of such maps as I had at hand'. The longitude of Liskeard had been 'determined from the observation of the transit of Venus in 1761, observed there by the Reverend Mr Haydon', Headmaster of Liskeard Grammar School.[43] Maskelyne entertained serious misgivings, 'suspecting that I might have been led into a mistake ... owing to the badness of the maps which I made use of' (see Figure 2). He expressed these doubts to the Board of Longitude, accompanied by a plea 'that some good astronomical observations might be made at the Lizard, in order to settle its true position'. The Board,

> being sensible of the importance of determining the position of a place of so much consequence in the British navigation, resolved that the proper astronomical observations should be made at the Lizard for that purpose.[44]

A particularly good opportunity to undertake these observations presented itself on the third day of June 1769 when the transit of Venus took place, followed the next morning by an eclipse of the Sun. Nevil Maskelyne observed these events at the Royal Observatory at Greenwich, and John Bradley (nephew of the late Dr Bradley, the third Astronomer Royal) was appointed to do the same at the Lizard. He stayed there from 13 May to 3 July, taking many observations with a variety of good instruments from a point north of a line joining the centres of the two lighthouses; the means of these many observations produced a latitude of 49°57'30"N. and a longitude from the Royal Observatory at Greenwich of 05°15'W.

It is clear that the position of the Lizard had, by the middle of the eighteenth century, become of scientific as well as navigational interest. Both interests remained active in the attempt to improve the co-ordinate determinations. The marine surveying undertaken by Murdoch Mackenzie (already alluded to as having taken place in 1773) was not published in chart form until the next century but the reasons for that and the fine tuning for the position of Lizard is another chapter in the blend of cartography and hydrography.

Acknowledgement

The author is deeply grateful for the generous help given to him by the Leverhulme Trust for the special object of continuing his work on the cartography of south-west England.

Notes

1 Lord Byron, *Don Juan* (1824), Canto IV, stanza 1.

2 A. Fox and W. Ravenhill, 'Old Burrow and Martinhoe', *Antiquity*, XXXIX (1965), 253-8. A. Fox and W. Ravenhill, 'Early Roman Outposts on the North Devon Coast, Old Burrow and Martinhoe', *Proceedings of the Devon Archaeological Exploration Society*, 24 (1966), 3-39.

3 B. Philp, *The Excavation of the Roman Forts of the Classis Britannica at Dover, 1970-77* (Dover Castle, Kent, 1981), 113.

4 R.M. Ogilvie and I. Richmond, eds, *Cornelii Taciti de Vita Agricolae* (Oxford, 1967), Cap.25 and p.239.

5 H. Cleeve, 'Roman Harbours in Britain south of Hadrian's Wall', in J. du Plat Taylor and H. Cleeve, eds, *Roman Shipping and Trade*, Council for British Archaeology (hereafter CBA), Research Report 24 (1978), 36-40. H. Cleeve, 'The Classis Britannica', in D.E. Johnston, ed., *The Saxon Shore*, CBA, Research Report 18 (1977), 16. M. Todd, 'The *Vici* of Western England' and H.D.H. Elkington, 'The Mendip Lead Industry', in K. Branigan and P.J. Fowler, eds, *The Roman West Country* (Newton Abbot, 1976), 99-119 and 183-97.

6 O.A.W. Dilke, *The Roman Land Surveyors* (Newton Abbot, 1971). O.A.W. Dilke, *Greek and Roman Maps* (1985).

7 C. Thomas, 'A Provisional List of Imported Pottery in Post-Roman Western Britain and Ireland', *Institute of Cornish Studies*, Special Report 7 (Redruth, 1981). C. Thomas, *Exploration of a Drowned Landscape* (1985), 149-99.

8 D.A.S. Peacock, 'The Rhine and the Problem of Gaulish Wine in Britain', in du Plat Taylor and Cleeve, eds, *Roman Shipping and Trade*, 41.

9 E.G. Bowen, *Saints, Seaways and Settlements in the Celtic Lands* (Cardiff, 1969). E.G. Bowen, *Britain and the Western Seaways* (1972).

10 J. Gairdner, ed., *Sailing Directions for the Circumnavigation of England and for a Voyage to the Straits of Gibraltar*, Hakluyt Society Publications (hereafter HS), 1st series, 79 (1889), 14. D.W. Waters, *The Rutters of the Sea* (New Haven & London, 1967), 19.

11 M.C. Andrews, 'The British Isles in the Nautical Charts of the Fourteenth and Fifteenth Centuries', *Geographical Journal* (hereafter *GJ*), 68 (1926), 474-81.

12 BL, Add. MS 19,510, ff.2v., 3.

13 J. Rotz, A Boke of Ydrographie, BL, Royal MS 20.E,IX; reproduced in facsimile in H. Wallis, ed., *The Maps and Text of the Boke of Ydrographie* (1982).

14 BL, Cotton MS Aug. I.i. 35, 36, 38 and 39.

15 J.H. Parry, *The Discovery of the Sea* (1975).

16 W. Bourne, *An Almanacke and Prognostication for Three Yeares ... 1571 and 1572 & 1573* (1571). This can conveniently be consulted in E.G.R. Taylor, ed., *A Regiment for the Sea and other Writings by William Bourne of Gravesend*, HS, (Cambridge, 1963), 91 and 271.

17 J. Dee, *General and Rare Memorials pertayning to the Perfect Arte of Navigation* (1577), 7.

18 L. J. Waghenaer, *De Spieghel der Zeevaerdt* (Leyden, 1584- 1585). Reproduced in facsimile with an Introduction by R.A. Skelton, *Theatrum Orbis Terrarum* (hereafter *TOT*), first series IV, (Amsterdam, 1964).

19 A. Ashley, *The Mariners Mirrovr* (1588). Reproduced in facsimile with an Introduction by R.A. Skelton, *TOT*, third series II, (Amsterdam, 1966).

20 W. Ravenhill, 'Christopher Saxton's Surveying: An Enigma', in S. Tyacke, ed., *English Map Making 1500-1650* (1983) 112-9.

21 W. Ravenhill, 'As to its Position in respect to the Heavens', *Imago Mundi*, 28 (1976), 83.

22 J. Green, *The Construction of Maps and Globes* (1717), 137.

23 D. Howse and M. Sanderson, *The Sea Chart* (Newton Abbot, 1973).

24 E. Wright, *Certaine Errors in Navigation* (1599).

25 W. Bourne, *An Almanacke ...* Preface to the Reader.

26 T. Campbell, 'The Drapers' Company and its School of Seventeenth Century Chart-makers', in H. Wallis and S. Tyacke, eds, *My Head is a Map* (1973), 81-106. T.R. Smith, 'Manuscript and Printed Sea Charts in Seventeenth Century London: The Case of the Thames School', in N.J.W.

Thrower, ed., *The Compleat Plattmaker* (Berkeley, Los Angeles, London, 1978), 45-100.

27 W. Ravenhill, 'Joel Gascoyne, – Cartographer', *Geographical Magazine* (1972), 335-41.

28 J.R. Tanner, ed., *Samuel Pepys Naval Minutes*, Navy Records Society, 60 (1926), 42, 237.

29 F.H. Blackburne Daniell, ed., *Calendar of State Papers Domestic Series, 1680-1681* (H.M.S.O., 1921), see also BL, Harleian MS 5946, f.202.

30 G. Collins, *Great Britain's Coasting Pilot* (1693).

31 Tanner, ed., *Pepys Naval Minutes*, 188-9.

32 W. Ravenhill, 'Joel Gascoyne, A Pioneer of Large-Scale County Mapping', *Imago Mundi*, 26 (1972), 60-70.

33 W. Ravenhill, 'Mapping the Lizard', *Map Collector*, 13 (1980), 29-36.

34 H. Moll, *A New Description of England and Wales* (1724), 1.

35 D. Pickering, *The Statutes at Large, XVII* (Cambridge, 1765), 466 and 467.

36 Letter from William Borlase to Charles Lyttleton, 3 May 1756. BL Stowe MS 752, f.176. The author is indebted to Peter Pool F.S.A. for calling his attention to this correspondence.

37 R. Heath, *A Natural and Historical Account of the Islands of Scilly* (1724), 450.

38 Now known as The Royal Society of Arts.

39 Royal Society of Arts, Guard Books I, 85, 11 February 1756. See also W. Ravenhill, *Benjamin Donn. A Map of the County of Devon 1765* (Exeter, 1965).

40 M. Mackenzie, *A Treatise of Maritim Surveying* (1774), xii. A.H.W. Robinson, *Marine Cartography in Britain* (Leicester, 1962).

41 Hydrographic Office, Taunton, 703. D.i.

42 The author is indebted to Lt Cdr D.W. Waters for alerting him to this Preface in the *Nautical Almanac* for 1769.

43 An Account of the Observations made on the Transit of Venus 6 June 1761 by the Rev. Mr Haydon. In a letter to John Bevis MD, dated Liskeard 9 June 1761. *Philosophical Transactions*, LII pt I (1761), 202-8.

44 N. Maskelyne, Preface to the *Nautical Almanac and Astronomical Ephemeris for the Year 1771* (1769).

THE IMPLICATIONS OF THE TIDAL RANGE

Alan Carr

I

There are a number of physical constraints which have influenced the maritime history of the peninsula of south-west England. These include the topography and structure of the land; coastal bathymetry and the nature of the sea bed; and a range of oceanographic factors mainly related to waves and tides. The purpose of this paper is to examine one single oceanographic parameter – that of tidal range – and some of its implications.

II

Dyer notes that the tidal range in the open ocean, the so-called Kelvin wave, is only of the order of 30cm; the rest is entirely due to the existence and form of land masses.[1] Figure 1 shows the mean spring tidal range, in metres, for the north and south coasts of Devon, together with adjacent areas, based on the *Admiralty Manual of Tides*.[2] In general, the values reflect the amplifying effects of the funnel-shaped Bristol Channel/Severn estuary in the north and the contrasting response to the more open southern coastline between Fowey and Portland. Thus, in the Bristol Channel, tidal range increases fairly progressively eastwards so that, at Avonmouth, the mean spring tidal range is 12.3m. However, on the south coast where the overall range is less, such changes as take place result in a relatively systematic diminution in the same eastwards direction. This reduction along the open coast is still more obvious outside the immediate area of concern, culminating in a range of only some 2.0m at the amphidromic point near Bournemouth,[3] though it should be noted that minimum range and minimum tidal current velocity do not always coincide. Tidal ranges are somewhat greater on equinoctial spring tides but correspondingly less on the fortnightly neap tides which alternate with ordinary springs. For example, at Plymouth (Devonport) the mean spring range is 4.7m but that of neaps is only 2.2m. Similarly, along the Bristol Channel coast the mean ranges at Ilfracombe and Avonmouth are reduced from 8.5 to 3.9m and 12.3 to 6.5m, respectively.

The values referred to so far reflect the ranges found on the relatively open coast. Where a river estuary occurs there are two conflicting tendencies: an increase due to convergence (eg the Bristol Channel) and a decrease due to

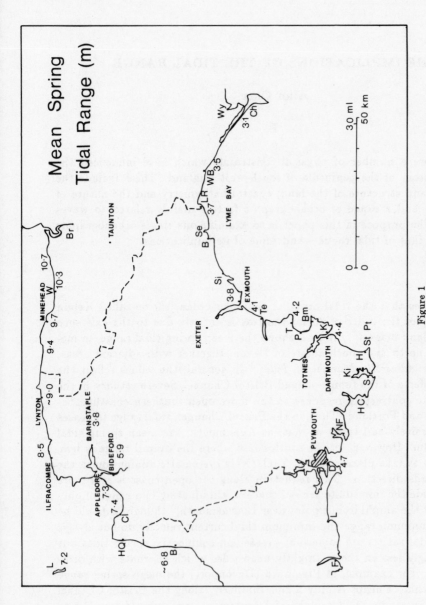

Figure 1

Devon and adjacent areas: Mean spring tidal range in metres.

Places shown as initials only are as follows: Beer, Devon (B); Bridgwater (Br); Brixham (Bm); Bude, Cornwall (B); Chiswell (Chesilton) (Ch); Clovelly (Cl); Devonport (D); Fowey (F); Hallsands (H); Hartland Quay (HQ); Hope Cove (HC); Kingsbridge (Ki); Kingswear (K); Looe (L); Lyme Regis (LR); Newton Ferrers (NF); Paignton (P); Salcombe (S); Seaton (Se); Sidmouth (Si); Start Point (St Pt); Teignmouth (Te); Torpoint (Plymouth) (T); Torquay (T); Watchet (W); West Bay, Bridport (WB); Weymouth (Wy). With the exception of Start Point all coastal locations shown on the map have, or had, harbour or landing

26

frictional losses of energy. The topographic and bathymetric form of the estuary is relevant in this context. The prime example of attenuation in Figure 1 is the Taw-Torridge estuary where the mean spring tidal range falls from 7.3m at Appledore to 5.9 and 3.8m at Bideford and Barnstaple respectively. This reduction in tidal range is also attributable, in some measure, to the freshwater flow from the upper reaches of each river. This has the effect of input throughout the whole tidal cycle, together with a countervailing current flow during the period of the rising tide. Another factor is the increasing elevation of the river bed upstream. While, in theory, the diminution in tidal range up-estuary provides certain logistic advantages, in practice these are outweighed by the short period at the top of the tide during which navigation is possible. Furthermore, freshwater input is variable reflecting previous precipitation events as modified by the run-off characteristics of the specific river drainage network.

In the open ocean the tidal curve is sinusoidal in form. Although the coastal configuration may modify this simple curve quite substantially in certain areas (eg the double high waters of Poole Harbour, Dorset, and the Isle of Wight) it has little effect on the north and south Devon shores. Thus, while the tidal range may differ from place to place and between spring and neap tides, the duration during which a given percentage of the maximum tidal level is reached remains much the same throughout. Table 1 lists the five nearest Standard Ports and gives the calculated duration of time that the tide level is at 80 per cent and 90 per cent of its mean spring tide maximum.

Table 1
Tidal Range and Tide Level in Selected Ports

Standard Port	Mean spring tidal range (metres)	Duration of time tide is within	
		80%	90%
		of maximum (minutes)	
Avonmouth	12.3	187	125
Swansea	8.6	220	155
Milford Haven	6.3	205	140
Devonport	4.7	255	170
Portland	1.9	210	145
Correlation:		-0.50	-0.53

Source: *Admiralty Tide Tables, 1985, Volume 1* (Taunton, 1984)

Although Table 1 suggests a weak, negative relation between tidal range and percentage duration, the correlation is not statistically significant, with Devonport, rather than Portland, having the longest duration. Therefore, while the tidal range is important in its effects, the duration is relatively immaterial from one location to another, although Devonport is marginally at an advantage relative to the other examples cited. Tidal velocities are more significant. Peregrine suggests that, in general, tidal current velocities have a close correlation to tidal height but that the phase may differ.[4] However, there are variations in detail, especially in estuaries. For example, Dyer provides a diagram of the Exe estuary which shows the marked tidal assymetry of depth mean velocities attributable to the covering and uncovering of the intertidal areas.[5]

The implications of tidal range are in harbour engineering; cargo handling; and ship design and handling. But the response is not necessarily the same under different economic circumstances. It seems pertinent therefore to examine the way not only the Devon coast, but also the north coast of the Bristol Channel, has responded to the environmental and temporal stimuli present. Swansea is particularly relevant in this context.

Harbour engineering and cargo-handling

Over the last 150 years general port design has progressed from cribs (logs, generally driven vertically and infilled with stone); through masonry or brick; to mass concrete, and finally to steel piles. In similar fashion breakwaters have developed from natural rock and rubble to the recent use of artificial, interlocking forms, such as tetrapods. The extent to which specific harbours reflect these phases is a combination of the intrinsic topographic opportunities and constraints, and the economic incentive for development. The precise timing of such stimuli is also germane in this context.

Where there is a large tidal range this has to be accommodated in one of three ways. In the first instance, small-scale works can be constructed when the tide is out, but the corollary to this is that only small craft may use the facilities and then at high water alone. Secondly, to provide access for more sizeable vessels with greater draught, and over a greater range of tidal height, much more substantial port engineering is required. This has to take the form of massive structures which allow larger vessels into harbour at or near high water but still afford protection when the tide is out. The third variant partly depends upon vessel design which may necessitate the construction of lock gates so that ships continue to be permanently afloat. These large-scale structures need to have their foundations near, at, or below low water mark yet have the quay level sufficiently high to provide for high spring tides plus an allowance for breaking storm waves and possible tidal surges. Thus capital costs may well be disproportionate to the opportunities for trade. Generally, locks have been built where extreme tidal ranges occur, providing the economic incentives existed, as at Barry, Cardiff and Swansea, but they are not necessarily restricted to sites with a very large tidal range as Millbay Docks, Plymouth, indicates.

In the specific instance of Swansea, Flower has noted that initially copper ore for smelting was supplied exclusively from Cornwall.[6] Primitive, but practical, flat-bottomed coasting vessels made the return voyage with coal. However, as demand for copper increased, ore was imported, mainly from Chile. This necessitated larger ocean-going vessels, and thus major port facilities began to be developed. In 1866, 17 out of 18 copper works in Britain were located in the Swansea area.[7] Similarly, tinplate exports grew from 12,000 in 1878 to 250,000 tons in 1885 and 547,000 tons approximately, including galvanised steel, in 1913. This represented three-quarters of UK production. Exports of coal and patent fuel through the port exceeded 5,000,000 tons at its peak. Ship movements increased from 694 entries in 1768, through 2,028 in 1793, to 5,745 in 1879. Overall traffic reached its peak in the 1950s with more than 10 million tons. Flower estimated the present-day replacement cost of the port of Swansea as of the order of £200 million.[8] No port in the south-west peninsula has approached this level of commercial activity.

Except where locks are present, the changing level of vessels over the tidal cycle relative to quay height presents problems in mooring, and loading and unloading, as does the often excessive distance between quay and ship deck. Drying out is an extreme variant of this phenomenon.

Ship design and handling

Large tidal range, and the drying out of harbours and estuaries at low water, has implications on ship design and handling. It also makes the question of a ship's draught and its clearance of the sea bed vis-a-vis the tide level particularly important. Flat-bottomed vessels had the double advantage that they could both be navigable over shallow bars at the mouths of estuaries such as the Taw-Torridge, and would also lie flat when dried out. Large tidal range is not necessarily a disadvantage if low water can be accommodated because high water allows large vessels. However, a smaller tidal range implies smaller vessels or substantial dredging to port approaches and ship's berths. The amount of cargo and/or the duration of stay in port are further considerations; thus, a fully or substantially-laden vessel may break her back upon drying out, while flooding may occur if water overtops the gunwale before the vessel refloats on the rising tide. Careful hull design, or the installation of drop or bilge keels in small craft, may obviate this problem but such features are often incompatible with other elements of ship design. As a consequence considerable numbers of ships are unable to use ports which dry out. An alternative solution is the use of lighterage with the off-loading or partial off-loading of large vessels outside the harbour or estuary. Apart from exposure to inclement weather there are substantial cost penalties in such double-handling. Other costs might accrue from the large tidal range in that time may be lost if a vessel misses a tide and is effectively confined within, or without, a port until the following high water. The fact that spring high waters are always at about the same time of day or night may be significant in the ease of ship-handling and the provision of port facilities.

Peregrine's assertion that the larger the tidal range the greater the tidal current velocities clearly has implications for ship-handling.[9] Thus, ship movements in the direction of tidal flow are more effective the greater the tidal range and passage times can be substantially reduced. In many respects this factor was, and is, of greater advantage to steam or diesel-powered vessels than to sailing ships since tidal velocities change rapidly over time and space, and manoeuverability may be rendered more difficult where rates are high. While a smaller tidal range would result in weaker tidal currents and hence slower vessel movement from this cause, it would enable tacking etc., to be more effectively and readily carried out.

III

This paper has dealt with general principles and only rarely, as in the cases of the Taw-Torridge estuary and Swansea, have specific locations been mentioned. Nevertheless, Figure 1 indicates most of the ports, harbours and landing places of Devon and the neighbouring coastline, together with representative spring tidal ranges. From these data it may be possible to attempt an assessment of the relevance of tidal range to harbour development at various places. It is apparent that while tidal range is important it is only one of a number of oceanographic parameters, such as exposure to wave attack, that influence siting and design. Furthermore, there are other physical constraints such as bathymetry and topography. When one considers the economic response to these diverse factors and their manifestations, there is already considerable scope for variation from place to place. Once other economic and other human considerations are added to this complex equation it is small wonder that each and every harbour and landing place is unique.

Notes

1 K.R. Dyer, *Coastal and Estuarine Sediment Dynamics* (Chichester, 1986), 89.

2 *Admiralty Tide Tables, 1985, Volume 1* (Taunton, 1984).

3 A.J. Lee and J.W. Ramster, eds, *Atlas of the Seas around the British Isles* (1981).

4 D.H. Peregrine, 'Tidal Currents', in M.L. Schwartz, ed., *Encyclopedia of Beaches and Coastal Environments* (Stroudsberg, Pennsylvania, 1982), 816.

5 Dyer, *Sediment Dynamics*, 243.

6 B.L. Flower, 'Dock and Harbour Planning, Maintenance and Development in relation to the Swansea Bay Ports', in M.A. Collins *et al,* eds, *Industrial Embayments and their Environmental Problems: A Case Study of Swansea Bay,* (Oxford, 1980), 565.

7 Flower, 'Dock and Harbour Planning', 567.

8 Flower, 'Dock and Harbour Planning', 571.

9 Peregrine, 'Tidal Currents', 816. It should be noted that slack water may well be slightly after high water rather than coincident with it.

CLIMATIC CHANGE AND THE HERRING AND PILCHARD FISHERIES OF DEVON AND CORNWALL

Alan Southward, Gerald Boalch and Linda Maddock

Introduction

The sea fisheries form a significant part of Devon's maritime history. Over the centuries the importance of different fisheries has altered, not only because of changes in human populations, or through improvements in catching and marketing, but as a result of variations in the natural environment. Fluctuations have been particularly apparent in the fisheries for herrings and pilchards, with the fish failing to arrive at the usual time, or in the normal abundance, in some years. In this preliminary contribution to an assessment of the marine resources of Devon we give a general view of fluctuations in the south-western pilchard and herring fisheries and indicate some of the natural factors influencing these fish.

Information on these fisheries comes from several sources, the most reliable data being provided by the official statistics on sea fisheries.[1] Collection of these statistics began in 1885, but in the early versions much of the data was aggregated, so that for species of fish, and the ports at which they were landed, the series begins in 1903 or 1905. Doubts have been cast about the accuracy of the fishery statistics, dependent as they are on the goodwill of fishermen and merchants. Moreover, the quality of the data and the means of presentation in printed form has changed over the years, sometimes at the whim of political pressures, so that gaps exist for some ports and certain fish. Nevertheless, the fishery statistics are invaluable; they provide the longest continuous time series of marine biological data, permitting a comparison with the MBA's series on the occurrence of the planktonic stages of fish off Plymouth, the .eggs and postlarvae, though this is only fully quantitative from 1924.

Fishery sources prior to 1903 are less satisfactory. Port Books offer details of cargoes, including those fish which were subject to tax or bounty, and occasionally of other fish landed. The series goes back to Elizabethan times, but is incomplete. Local newspapers constitute another primary source, with accounts of fish catches or landings at the ports, and occasional general comments about the relative success of the fishery. However, for considerable stretches of the past 400 years it is necessary to use secondary sources, particularly the informed comment of natural historians, and the work of local historians; other secondary sources are the various 'surveys' and 'county histories', and the more general accounts by travel writers who visited the South

West. The earlier travelogues and natural histories give more details of the pilchard fishery than the herring fishery, largely because travellers from up-country found pilchards a new experience, while local authors were impressed by their economic significance.[2]

The Environmental Background

Devon lies near the boundary between the shallow turbid waters eastward up the English and Bristol Channels, and the open, deeper waters to the west. Along the English Channel coast the waters to the east are vertically mixed, while to the west, and in part of Lyme Bay, they are stratified in summer, when a layer of warm water overlies a larger mass of much colder water. This layering separates warm-water life in the surface waters from colder water life closer to the bottom. In winter the lines of equal salt content and temperature tend to run parallel with the south coast, and the centre of the Channel shows a tongue of warm saline water penetrating from the west up channel. In contrast, on the north coast, the isolines for temperature and salinity tend to run at right angles to the land so that, in winter, the water of the Bristol Channel gets colder, less saline and more turbid further to the east, as Figure 1 shows. This difference is due largely to the enclosed nature and fierce tidal streams of the Bristol Channel, as opposed to the slower flow through the English Channel into the North Sea. The south-western peninsula also lies at a natural biogeographic boundary between marine life adapted to conditions in the colder water farther north, and other forms of life adapted to warmer water conditions to the south.

As a result of these environmental complexities the seas off Devon and Cornwall yield a very diverse catch of fishes that includes cold-water and warm-water species. Fishes can be divided into two main groups according to whether they usually feed close to the sea bed, and are caught there, or whether they feed in mid-water and are captured in mid-water nets. The latter group are usually denoted pelagic fish, whereas it is the demersal species that stay close to the bottom. This is a rough and ready division, since many pelagic fish, including herring and mackerel, may remain close to the sea bed in day-time; however, it does recognise the difference in catching techniques. There are five dominant species of pelagic fish in the waters off Devon – pilchard, herring, sprat, mackerel, and horse-mackerel. The last spends more time near the bottom than the rest, while the sprat is small and is taken using a very different catching technique. Of the three remaining species, mackerel are differentiated by their greater readiness to go for larger food prey, and they are the only fish in the group that are regularly taken with spinners or feathers, hooks disguised to look like the smaller fish on which they prey. The two remaining pelagic fish, herring and pilchard, are closely related. Both species feed mostly on plankton, and therefore compete for the same or similar food resource, while they are both captured by similar methods, though fishing techniques have changed over time. Whereas, in the present day, the herring and pilchard fisheries are prosecuted with trawls towed in mid-water, or with

34

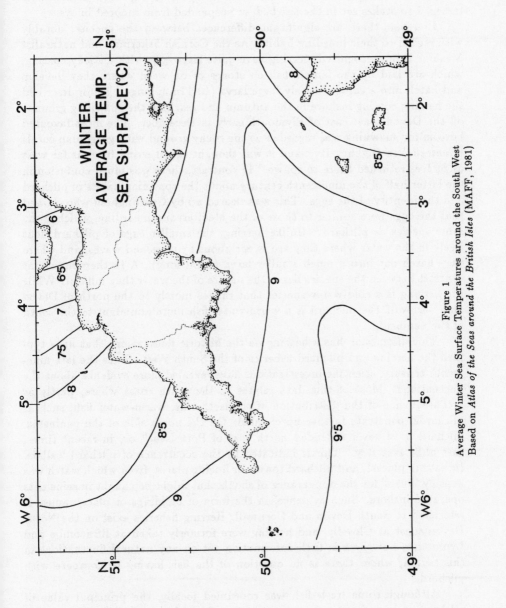

Figure 1

Average Winter Sea Surface Temperatures around the South West
Based on *Atlas of the Seas around the British Isles* (MAFF, 1981)

purse seines used to enclose large shoals, in the early twentieth century they were taken passively in drift nets. Before 1830 the bulk of the pilchard catch had been taken in seines operated close inshore from a group of small boats, while a small proportion of herrings have always been captured in fixed nets fastened to stakes set in the sea bed, or suspended from moored buoys.

However, there are significant differences between the species, notably with regard to their breeding habits. As the Cornish fisherman and naturalist Mathias Dunn recognised, herring have quite large eggs with a sticky coating, which are laid by the female fish on stones or on weed where they develop and hatch into a comparatively large larva (10-11mm long).[3] Dunn described the herring coming inshore in the autumn and reaching the spawning grounds off the Devon coast east of Plymouth early in December. The most favoured bottom for spawning was regarded as the rocky ground with gorgonian corals (*Eunicella*) in Bigbury Bay, and it was thought that herring from as far west as St Ives returned there to spawn.[4] In contrast, there was much confusion in the latter half of the nineteenth century about the spawning habits of pilchard and the identity of the eggs. This was cleared up by Cunningham who showed that the eggs were similar to those of the Mediterranean sardine, which is the same species as pilchard.[5] Unlike herring, the smaller eggs of pilchard float freely in the water where they are swept about by tides and waves, and where they hatch out into a much smaller larva (4mm long). A further important contrast between the species lies in the nature of the water they inhabit. While the herring is a cold-water species that ranges mostly to the north of Devon and Cornwall, the pilchard is a warm-water fish more abundant to the south of the peninsula.

This distinction has a bearing on the historic fluctuations that have typified the herring and pilchard fisheries of the South West. Since the late nineteenth century, scientific investigations have revealed more evidence about the fluctuations. Most of this data relates to the south coast where, partly as a consequence of the distribution of the isotherms, warm-water fish, such as pilchards, penetrate further up channel. On the north side of the peninsula, pilchard have never extended north east of Port Isaac[6] or, in recent times, east of St Ives Bay.[7] This is indicated by the occurrence of pilchard 'cellars' (ie salting places), and pilchard towers or hueing places, from which watch was kept by 'huers' for the appearance of shoals that might be caught in seine nets operated inshore. Such evidence, in the form of buildings or place names, is restricted to South Devon and Cornwall. Herring fisheries exist on the North Devon coast at Clovelly, and herring were formerly taken at Ilfracombe and Lynmouth, but there is little information yet on any natural fluctuations in this region, where there is no question of the fish having to compete with pilchard.

Although some fresh fish was consumed locally, the principal value of pilchard and herring lay in the ease with which they could be preserved for domestic consumption or for the export market. Both were salted,[8] though until the seventeenth century pilchards were smoked and dried, the cured product being dubbed 'fumados',[9] or 'fair maids' in Devon dialect. Thereafter, and until the 1950s, pilchards were subjected to a fairly standard curing process.[10] Initially, they were stacked and salted dry for between 24 and 48 hours, some of the oil draining out at this stage; excess salt was then removed and the fish carefully pressed in open barrels to remove the rest of the oil before closing the staves and sealing. The pilchard oil ('trayne' or train oil), was a valuable by-product which was exported and used for many purposes including the manufacture of lead paint. In recent times, most of the pilchards caught by purse-seining have been transported by road from the South West for conversion into fish meal.

Fluctuations in the Pilchard and Herring Fisheries of South Devon and south-east Cornwall before 1900

Fish was afforded a great economic importance in Tudor times. Two, sometimes three 'fish-days' a week were enforced by legislation aimed at increasing the size of the fishing fleet, thereby lessening dependence on imports, and providing a supply of trained seamen to be drawn upon in time of war.[11] These concerns, together with the taxation of pilchards to pay for Plymouth's defences, and disputes regarding the grants of monopolies to favoured courtiers,[12] have generated much of the early evidence about the fishery.

The season of the fishery, rather than its yield, is the subject of most of the older accounts. Jonathan Couch, the Polperro naturalist, citing the ledgers of Richard Trevill, commented that the fishery commenced in August in 1597, and in July the following year.[13] In the early seventeenth century, Norden noted that 'pilchards...aboundeth upon the sea coast (of Cornwall) ...especially in the south parte...between St Jeame's tide and the feast of All Saynts', or from late June to the end of October.[14] Whetter's analysis of the Port Books suggests that the pilchard fishery continued to be profitable in Cornwall and South Devon during the first half of the seventeenth century, the fish appearing 'fairly regularly along the whole coast from Bolt Head to St Ives'. Later in the century, pilchard appear to have been much scarcer, with the export trade of Plymouth suffering a marked decline; moreover, the greatest number were caught off West Cornwall, 'from Fowey westwards', while the season occurred progressively later, even as late as January off Mevagissey in 1671.[15] The Devon Port Books also suggest a transformation in the seventeenth century, with Dartmouth's considerable export trade in cured pilchards in the early part of the Stuart era declining markedly after mid-century. On the other hand, the evidence suggests that a considerable coastal trade in pickled herrings took place in the seventeenth century along the north coast of the peninsula, with a definite increase in its east-west flow in the second half of the century.[16] The south coast's herring trade also increased during the period of diminishing pilchard yields, with considerable exports of cured herring recorded from as far west as Mount's Bay after 1675.[17] Thus, the available evidence indicates that a westward retreat of the pilchards along the south coast of Devon and Cornwall in the second half of the seventeenth century was accompanied by an abundance of herrings on both coasts of the peninsula; significantly, this was a period of relatively cold climatic conditions.

There is little direct data on the relative abundance of pilchards and herrings in the eighteenth century. The impressionistic evidence, however, suggests that the pilchard fishery recovered in the first quarter of the century, Defoe describing a fishery at Dartmouth as well as in Cornwall.[18] Later in the century, the travelogues mention only the Cornish fishery,[19] while in 1797 Polwhele concurred in stating that pilchards had been much more abundant in previous times,[20] and Bellamy noted the total absence of the fishery from the Cornish coast in 1786 and 1787.[21] In 1794, Maton came to a similar conclusion remarking that 'ten years ago...the fish were so scarce that the families of the fishermen lived solely on limpets'.[22] A revival in the pilchard fishery is apparent after 1800, with fish being taken off Dawlish and Teignmouth, and also in Start Bay, while the Bigbury Bay fishery flourished in the years 1811-1817, large numbers of pilchards being captured in seine nets and cured on Borough Island, and at the mouth of the Avon.[23] In 1843, however, Bellamy noted the abandonment of the Bigbury Bay fishery which had 'failed for the last eight years',[24] a failure which was subsequently repeated in Whitesand Bay, and then at Menabilly.[25] Witnesses at the 1865 Royal Commission, indicated that the decline in pilchard abundance was accompanied by an increase in herring fishing,[26] the change in Plymouth Sound resulting from the construction of the Breakwater according to some authorities.[27] More objective information is provided by the Yeovil newspaper *Pulman's Weekly News*, which recorded details of herring, mackerel and pilchard catches in Torbay and Lyme Bay from the 1850s. An analysis of the 1857-85 period, reveals that the mackerel fishery of East Devon was virtually certain each summer, but the pilchard and herring fisheries were much more variable, with pilchard apparently more numerous in the middle years of the century, and herring more abundant in the later years.[28]

Fluctuations are also apparent in the seasonality of the pilchard and herring fisheries. In 1822, Couch pointed out that

for upwards of thirty years, at the middle of the last century, the most successful portion of the [pilchard] fishery was carried on after the autumn equinox, and consequently by drift nets...But towards the end of the same century a change took place, and the principal success was from the beginning of August to the end of September. It is now found that after a nearly equal extent of time the winter fishery along the southward coast is alone or chiefly successful.[29]

In presenting evidence to the Royal Commission in 1865, Couch gave more detail:

in my recollection...the season at which pilchard was caught was different from what it is now. There has been a change in the time of carrying on the pilchard fishery from summer to winter. About 30 to 40 years ago the principal fishing for pilchards was in August and September. Since that time it appears to have dropped back again into October and November and perhaps December and January; and

38

so it appears to have been in earlier times. There were intervals of between 30 and 40 years of that sort of transition. There are records of such a transition having taken place two or three times before.[30]

Other commentators noted a similar pattern; in 1794, Maton, for instance, stated that 'the time at which the pilchards made their appearance is about the middle of July; at the latter end of September they depart. Thirty or forty years back Christmas was the time of their departure'.[31] Bellamy also noticed changes and irregularities in the time of the fishery, which normally commenced in August and continued to the end of September, but in 1837 the fish did not come in until November, in 1838 it was October, while in 1840 and 1842 pilchard were apparent in December and January.[32]

Fluctuations were also observed in the time of herring fishing, as Couch indicated briefly to the 1865 Royal Commission. At this time small herrings were around all year, but the fishery was concentrated mainly in October and November, sometimes extending into January and February. Bellamy confirmed these periods, noting that herrings were apparent in inshore waters in November and December, with lean, spent fish in January.[33] These fish were taken in drift nets, and though herrings may well have been present at other times of the year, the shoals were probably too small to be captured by drifting.

The variable seasonality of the pilchard and herring fisheries is not easy to explain. In Dunn's opinion, there were two races of herring in the South West, of different origins; thus, 'the small herring spawns in December and January, and the larger in March and sometimes early in April'.[34] Similarly, Couch was convinced that there were two seasons of pilchard spawning, with peaks in April and October, the spring group spawning farther offshore. There were differences in distribution of fat reserves in the muscle and the mesenteries, he argued, which suggested that these two spawning groups were different fish.[35] Other Cornish naturalists also opined that there were two lots of pilchard, early and late spawners; Dunn subscribed to this view, and in recognising the warm-water nature of the pilchard species, suggested that the fish had its winter quarters in the deeper water of the Channel, and eschewed shallow water where it might suffer from lower temperatures.[36] Certainly, the long term evidence suggests that there were two seasons of pilchard fishing, one in late summer and early autumn which formed the main fishery in the 1590s and from 1800 to 1835, and the other in late autumn and winter, as occurred in the late eighteenth century and the period 1860-1890. However, it is not yet clear whether these different fisheries were exploiting the same autumn-spawning fish which were appearing off the coast at different times, or if the summer fishery was prosecuted on the pilchard population that spawns in spring and early summer.

Herring and Pilchard Abundance since 1900

Data supplied by sailing drifters working off Devon and Cornwall in the period 1895-1911 suggest a change in the relative abundance of pelagic fish from east to west.[37] In East Devon, 99 per cent of the catch was herring, while in West Cornwall pilchard was the dominant species, though 17 per cent of the catch was herring. After 1900, these drifters took some pilchards off South Devon in July and August as well as in October and November, and the principal Cornish fishery peaked in August and September. Such figures indicate a shift away from the winter fishery of the late nineteenth century. Official statistics of the landings of herrings and pilchards at south-western ports are available from 1903, permitting a comparison of the fisheries of these ports, as Figure 2 illustrates. For the purposes of this paper, the experience of two major ports – Plymouth and Brixham – and one lesser base, Beer is instructive. The Plymouth data suggest that the local herring fishery was relatively stable in the first quarter of the twentieth century, but that a large increase in landings occurred between 1922 and 1934. In part, this expansion may be explained by an increase in the abundance of herrings, for the catch at Beer also increased at this time. However, the primary reason was an increase in the size of the fishing fleet as large numbers of steam drifters, most of which were registered at Lowestoft and Yarmouth, visited Plymouth at the peak of the season, in December and January. Indeed, from 1926, it seems that the fish actually became scarcer, for the output per vessel fell, the high yields being sustained by a growing number of boats.

In the 1930s, the Plymouth herring fishery suffered a drastic decline. Post-war investigation of the fishery data revealed that 'recruitment' – the survival of the young fish to enter the fishery in three years as maturing juveniles – had totally failed. Thus, from 1930 to 1936, when the fishery finally collapsed, the catch was dependent on surviving fish from previous years' successful spawnings, and by 1936 all the remaining fish were more than six years old.[38] Beer also witnessed a decline in herring catches from 1930 to 1936, though some fish survived, and small landings were recorded up to the outbreak of the Second World War. It would appear that the winter pilchard fishery also suffered during the 1930s, though catches were landed at Beer in the early 1940s, when no herrings were apparent.[39]

After 1945, when drift netting resumed, catches of herring were almost negligible at both Beer and Plymouth, and such activity ceased. Drifting for pilchards off Plymouth continued a little longer, with some landings in the mid-1950s, though this had also ceased by 1960. Landings of herring at Brixham were always smaller than those at Plymouth, and fluctuated widely from year to year, as Figure 3 shows. The fishery generally occurred in the autumn, earlier than the Plymouth fishery. Landings declined in the 1930s, but the fishery resumed after the Second World War, and though the collapse of the 1950s appeared final, there has been a small revival of herring landings at Brixham in recent years. On the other hand, pilchards have always played a minor role at Brixham and no definite trend can be discerned. However, in the South West in general, the revival of the mackerel fishery in the late 1960s led to a brief resumption of the winter pilchard fishery, though this declined as the mackerel boats deserted the region in the 1980s.

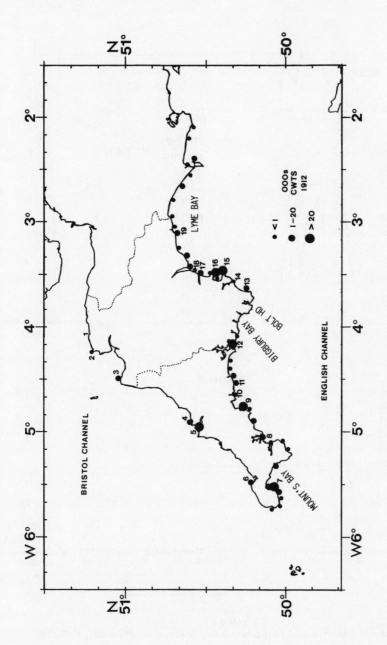

Figure 2

South-western Fishing Ports by Total Weight of Fish Landed in 1912

1 Lynmouth 2 Ilfracombe 3 Clovelly 4 Port Isaac 5 Padstow 6 St Ives 7 Newlyn 8 Falmouth 9 Mevagissey
10 Fowey 11 Polperro 12 Plymouth 13 Start Bay 14 Dartmouth 15 Brixham 16 Torquay 17 Teignmouth
18 Dawlish 19 Beer

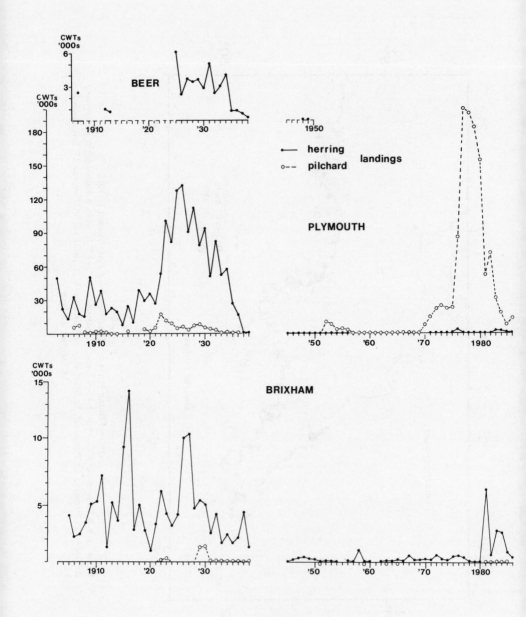

Figure 3
Annual Landings of Herrings and Pilchards at Beer, Brixham, and Plymouth, 1903-1986
Note that different scales are used for each port

42

Despite the failure of the winter pilchard fishery in the 1930s, there is ample evidence to indicate an increased abundance of pilchards off south-east Cornwall and South Devon from 1930. Weekly plankton samples taken off Plymouth since 1924 showed pilchard eggs to be very abundant in spring and summer after 1934, pointing to very big increases in the fish several years earlier. These summer pilchard were scarcely fished at all, hence we have to rely on the egg abundance to build up a picture of their numbers. Working from the eggs and the fecundity of the females, there were estimated to be about 30,000 mature pilchards below each square mile of the Channel in the 1950s, a much higher figure than could be estimated for all pelagic fish, including herring, before 1930.[40] Thus, there had been no real decline in fertility of the sea in the western English Channel as had been thought at the time,[41] rather the reverse. Figure 4 illustrates the seasonal changes in pilchard eggs off Plymouth and shows the separation into spring/summer and autumn spawners. It was only the spring/summer spawning stock of pilchards that increased at the time the herring fishery failed; the autumn eggs were present in more or less the same numbers as before, much less than the summer eggs. Annual changes in the two groups of pilchard eggs since the 1920s are shown in Figure 5. The massive increase in eggs of the summer spawners continued, with fluctuations, right through to the 1960s when the autumn spawners showed signs of increase. The summer eggs then declined and for some years in the 1970s there was virtually no spawning of pilchards off Plymouth in spring/summer and the revived winter fishery was based on the autumn spawning pilchards.[42] The role of dominant pelagic fish had by this time been taken over by the mackerel. It has only been in the last few years, after the disappearance of large mackerel shoals, that pilchard eggs have again begun to increase in number during summer.

These twentieth-century patterns – the relative insignificance of pilchard landings at Brixham and in East Devon, and the survival there of some herring fishing after the collapse of Plymouth's fishery – underlines the evidence provided by the sailing drifters; this suggested that the two species have opposing abundance trends, pilchard being dominant to the west, and herring to the east of Plymouth. Over time, further patterns can be detected; thus, the flourishing herring population of the 1920s and early 1930s was replaced by summer pilchards in the waters off Plymouth, though this was not the case elsewhere, while, in the west, the traditional winter pilchard fishery became unreliable. In the 1960s, a decline in summer pilchard abundance was not accompanied by an increase in herring abundance, though mackerel became very numerous, and there were good catches of winter pilchards.

Climate and the Herring and Pilchard Fisheries

The evidence regarding the relative abundance of herring and pilchard over the last 400 years suggests that the two species tended to alternate, with pilchard abundant at times when herring were scarce, and vice-versa. It was Cunningham who first advanced such a hypothesis; thus,

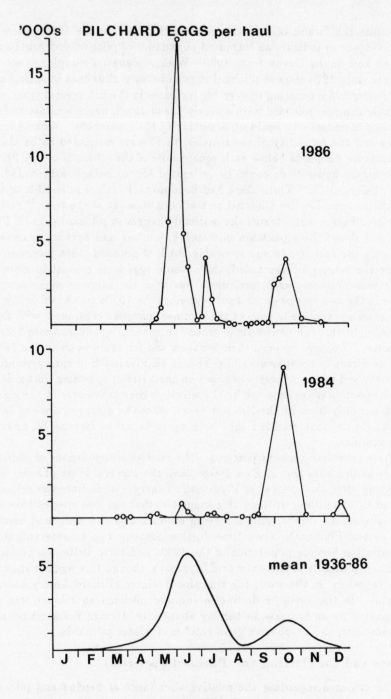

Figure 4
Pilchard Spawning Seasons at Plankton Station L5 (off Plymouth)
The 1936-1986 mean is compared with 1984, a year with an autumn maximum;
and with 1986, a year with spring and summer maxima

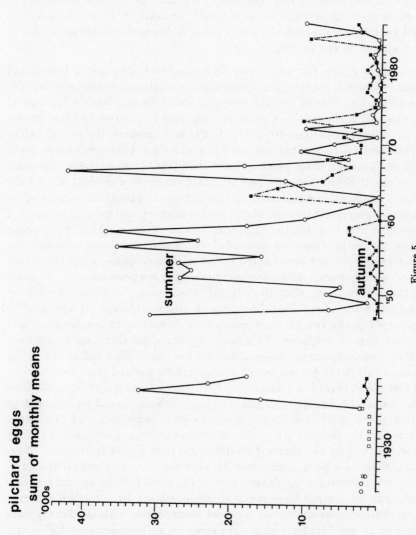

Figure 5

Pilchard Egg Abundance at Plankton Station L5 (off Plymouth)

The monthly means have been summed for 'summer' (April to July) and for 'autumn' (September to December)

it would appear that there is on the north coast of Cornwall an alternation of pilchard periods and herring periods, and it is natural to surmise that this is due to some alternating change in the physical conditions of the sea. As the Cornish coasts form the northern limit of the range of the pilchard, it seems possible that in certain periods the drift of warm water from the south extends further to the north, and that the pilchard then extends its wanderings ... while in other periods the drift of warm water is weaker or takes another direction, and that for this reason the north coast is deserted by the pilchard and visited by the herring.[43]

In this seminal statement, which can be applied to the coasts of Devon and Cornwall in general, Cunningham points to the relationship between the occurrence of the two species and the temperature of the sea, itself a function of the climate. This climatic link is clearly apparent in the two extreme phases of fish abundance in the last 400 years. In the first instance, the second half of the seventeenth century witnessed a marked scarcity of pilchards except in the far west of Cornwall, while herrings were abundant. More recently, it is clear that between 1930 and 1960 summer pilchards were very abundant around the south-west peninsula, as indicated by the increase in planktonic eggs, and by echo-sounder surveys,[44] but the winter pilchard fishery was unsatisfactory, and herrings were also very scarce. Significantly, these eras in which one or other of the species was predominant, coincided with long-run climatic extremes, the late seventeenth century being noted for its relative coolness, while the period 1930-1960 was characterised by comparatively high sea temperatures. At other times, there were lesser alterations in fish abundance. To establish whether these minor oscillations varied directly with climatic change, as appeared to have occurred in the two extreme instances, information on sea temperatures in previous times is required. This poses problems, for there are no continuous inshore sea temperature observations for the South West before the 1880s. However, a substitute for sea temperatures can be derived from two sources. In the first place, there is a relationship between air temperature over the land and sea temperature inshore. In our area this relationship can be obscured by advection of oceanic (warm) water from the west and south west in autumn and winter, by the lag that is introduced due to the large specific heat capacity of sea water, and by the thermal stratification that occurs in summer. Nevertheless, there is a good correlation between seasonal and annual trends in air and sea temperatures, as Table 1 shows. Plausible inshore annual sea temperatures can be derived from mean air temperatures by a correction factor based on regression analysis, but for most comparisons with the fishery data it is simpler to use Manley's long term series of air temperatures for central England, updated as suggested by Lamb.[45]

Secondly, a relationship also appears to exist between solar activity and climate (including local sea temperature). It is common knowledge that the disc of the sun carries dark patches on it, the so-called sunspots, which wax and wane. The number of sunspots undergoes a cyclic alternation, showing

Table 1

Correlation between Annual Values of Air Temperature and Inshore Sea Temperature at various localities

	A	B	C	D	E	F	G	
A	–	.74	.52	.81	.72	.74	.10	
B	.80	–	.52	.70	.68	.61	.37	
C	.53	.33	–	.43	.43	.53	.39	Annual
D	.90	.82	.48	–	.78	.91	.15	Means
E	.59	.69	.43	.65	–	.78	.07	
F	.82	.81	.54	.92	.65	–	.11	
G	.28	.55	.58	.33	.14	.24	–	

5-year running means

Key

A Plymouth sea surface, 1898-1986
B E1 sea surface (25 nautical miles south of Plymouth 1903- 1986)
C Biscay sea surface 1854-1984
D Plymouth air 1871-1986
E Guernsey air 1843-1878
F Central England air 1659-1984
G Sunspots 1700-1986

Values of correlation co-efficient (r) greater than 0.5 indicate more than 25 per cent in common; over 0.71 more than 50 per cent in common. The upper half of the table is for simple annual means, the lower half for smoothed (5-year running) means.

maxima approximately 11 years apart. In the past much nonsense has been written about other cycles (e.g. of business activity and crime) that appear to synchronize with the sunspots, but recently it has become clear that the sunspots are but external manifestations of real changes in the sun that influence radiation reaching the earth; moreover superimposed on the 11-year cycle there are longer cycles of 22-, 45-, 90-, and 180-year periods, some of them apparently related to planetary movements and therefore predictable.[46] The recent period of pilchard abundance and higher sea temperatures from 1930 to 1960 coincided with one of the longer term peaks of sunspot activity, while the cold period at the end of the seventeenth century had a minimum of sunspot activity. These two periods represent the maximum and minimum of the past 500 years in sunspots, temperature, and pilchard abundance. Reasonable records of sunspot counts are available back to the seventeenth century,[47] and it has been possible to take the more fragmentary records from earlier periods and construct possible cycles by adjustment against tree ring widths and their content of Carbon-14, which are known to be synchronized to more recent solar cycles.[48]

Figure 6 is constructed from such sources, and also shows what is known of the changes in the pilchard and herring before 1700. Figures 7 and 8 show average annual temperatures for central England since the mid-seventeenth century compared with summaries of the herring/pilchard fluctuations already described. The fit of the smaller fluctuations is not as good as it might be if we had more quantitative data on the fisheries and better records of local sea temperature. Nevertheless, it is enough to confirm the presence of a relationship over most of the 400 years being considered. What we may regard as the normal situation over the last 400 years in Devon and Cornwall is the co-existence of fisheries for herrings and pilchards along the south coast, the herrings predominant to the east, and pilchards to the west. In contrast, on the north coast, the herring fishery is dominant, with pilchards found only at the western tip of Cornwall. In warm periods the pilchard fishery extends up Channel to the South Hams and Lyme Bay along the south coast and towards Port Isaac on the north coast; in very warm periods the winter fishery is unreliable and more fish are available in summer. In cold periods, the pilchard fishery becomes progressively later in the autumn so that seining from small boats, which requires good weather, becomes unprofitable; and in really cold periods the fish occur only off West Cornwall. The herring fishery flourishes better in really cold periods and then extends farther to the west along the south coast; in warm periods, the herring is less abundant, leading to the impoverishment of the South Devon herring fishery, as occurred in the middle decades of the present century.

Having established this relationship, it is pertinent to assess how temperature influences the relative abundance of the two species, and whether the apparent solar relationship can be used to predict future trends. In earlier attempts to relate fluctuations in pelagic fish catches directly to the sunspot cycle, or solar activity, the fits tended to be unconvincing, or the absence of a plausible linking mechanism detracted from their value.[49] However, studies of the alternation of herring and pilchard off Plymouth in the 1930s form a base for further enquiry into the mechanism of the link with climate. Cushing, apparently unaware of Cunningham's hypothesis, attributed the failure of the Plymouth herring fishery to increased competition with pilchard; he showed some convincing statistical correlation between the decline and pilchard egg abundance, suggesting also that a (deduced) increase in juvenile pilchards could explain the coincidental changes in dissolved nutrients in the sea, particularly phosphorus. Thus, the difference in the winter level of phosphate between the 1920s and the 1930s represented the amount of the element 'locked up' in the larger, overwintering population of young pilchard.[50]

Southward, also unaware of Cunningham's hypothesis, adopted Cushing's theory of competition between herring and pilchard, but pointed out that this was just one aspect of a general ecological change that had occurred off Plymouth in the 1930s. Other pairs of competing species had shown the same

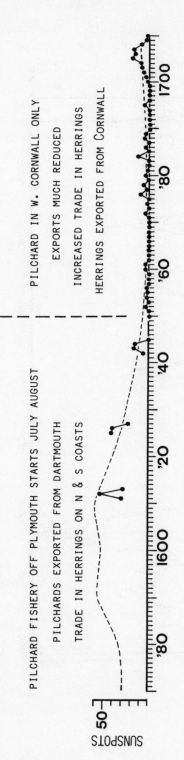

Figure 6

Sunspot Indices Related to Herring and Pilchard Abundance in the South West, 1570-1710

The dots show corrected annual values from observations. The broken line is the average for each 11-year cycle and is derived from the late 17th-century observations, or from estimates of tree ring carbon-14 values, after Eddy, 'Maunder Minimum'

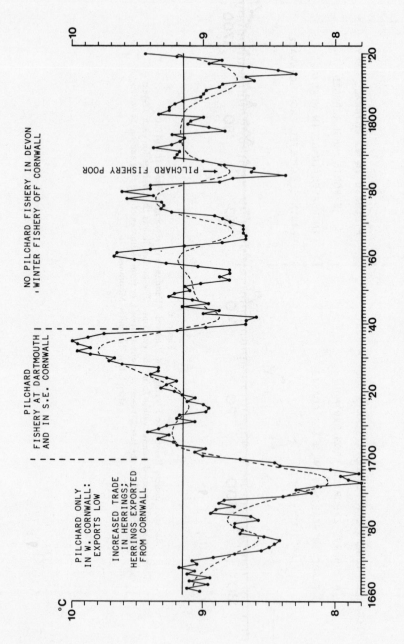

Figure 7

Central England Air Temperatures Related to Herring and Pilchard Abundance in the South West, 1659-1820
The temperatures are 5-year running means; the broken line shows the long-term trend as a smoothed fit to
the 11-year running means. Based on Manley, 'Central England Temperatures'

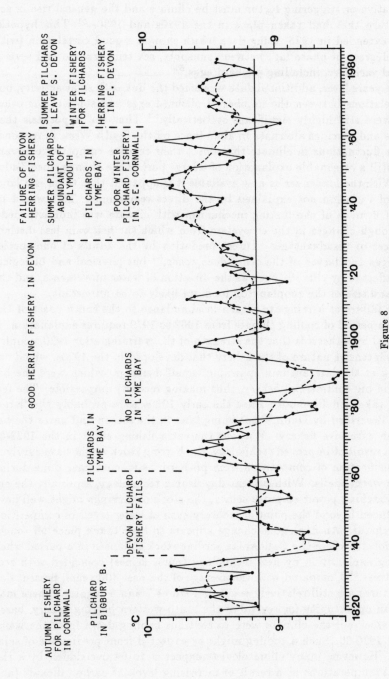

Figure 8

Central England Air Temperatures Related to Herring and Pilchard Abundance in the South West, 1820-1985
The temperatures are 5-year running means; the broken line shows the long-term trend as a smoothed fit to
the 11-year running means. Based on Manley, 'Central England Temperatures', adjusted according to Lamb,
Climate. Past, Present and Future

changes whereby a warm-water species had increased at the expense of a cold-water species. With such a general change taking place it was suggested that the causative or triggering factor must be climate and the general rise in sea temperature that had taken place in the 1920s and 1930s.[51] This hypothesis was extended in 1975, using data which showed a good correlation (with varying degrees of phase lag) between sunspots, sea temperature and several biological variables, including pilchard eggs.[52]

Five years later, additional data weakened the link with solar activity, but the correlations between the number of pilchard eggs and some of the other factors were still highly significant statistically.[53] Thus the hypothesis that pilchards and herrings alternate in abundance off the South West, in response to minor fluctuations in climate that affect their relative competitive advantage, is still a reasonable explanation of a large part of the change since Tudor times. With the longer series now available it is apparent that there is a large residue of variation not explained by the direct regressions. This would be expected if much of the linking mechanism with climate was indirect, mediated through changes in the ecosystem from which the fish gain less distinct advantages or disadvantages. Direct predation by the adults of one species on the eggs and larvae of the other does occur,[54] but physical and biological factors affected by climate, such as the direction of water movements, and the species and size of the zooplankton food are likely to be important.

The failure of herrings to return in abundance to the south coast of Devon in the period of cooling climate from 1962 to 1979 requires explanation. A provisional hypothesis is that the strength of the warming after 1920, coupled with the intensive nature of the fishery that developed in the 1920s, wiped out the stock of the late autumn spawning 'small' herrings, which were the basis for the big commercial fishery, thus making recovery impossible. The few herrings taken off Plymouth since the early 1960s were probably the 'large' herrings described by Dunn,[55] spawning later in the season and never the basis for an extensive fishery. Without the extra fishing effort in the 1922-34 period, a result of improved technology, the herring stock might have survived the intensification of competition from pilchard, as it must have done during previous warm spells. With present-day fishing technology, especially the enhanced catching power of purse seines, the stock of herrings might well have been reduced beyond the point of recovery even at lesser levels of competition from pilchards. An analagous change appears to have taken place off southern California, where the Californian sardine stock collapsed in a period when increasing exploitation by new technology (purse seines) coincided with ecological stress.[56] Compared with the average of the past 400 years, present day temperatures are still relatively warm as Figures 7 and 8 suggest. There may still be an opportunity for revival of the south-western herring fishery, based on new stocks, if the climate were to continue cooling down from the warm phase of 1930-60. Such a cooling might be expected from predictions of solar activity. However, many climatologists expect it to be overridden by a rise in global temperatures as a result of increasing levels of carbon dioxide (and fluorocarbon and other gases) emitted into the atmosphere by man's activities

– the so-called 'greenhouse effect'[57] – in which case pilchards will continue to benefit at the expense of herrings.

Conclusion

It is clear from a variety of sources that the herring and pilchard fisheries of the South West have fluctuated according to the relative abundance of the two species. A significant part of these fluctuations, which have been apparent since the sixteenth century, can be explained by temperature change, with the pilchard fishery flourishing in relatively warm periods, and the herring fishery more extensive in cooler eras. This has been so especially along the south coast of Devon and Cornwall where the two species have tended to alternate in abundance in accord with long-run climatic fluctuations. It would seem that temperature change has had an indirect impact, affecting the competitive advantage of the two species through related physical and biological factors, notably the species and size of zooplankton food, and the direction of water movements.

Notes

1 *Annual Reports of Proceedings under Acts relating to Sea Fisheries (England and Wales)*, Board of Agriculture (HMSO, 1903-18); *Sea Fisheries Statistical Tables (England and Wales)*, Ministry of Agriculture and Fisheries (HMSO, 1919-66); *Monthly Returns of Sea Fisheries (England and Wales)*, Ministry of Agriculture, Fisheries, and Food (MAFF Fisheries Statistics Unit, 1967-84).

2 For instance, see W. Borlase, *The Natural History of Cornwall* (Oxford, 1758). Borlase related that cured pilchards exported from Cornwall in 1747-56 averaged 29,975 hogsheads per annum, valued at £49,532 before bounty.

3 M. Dunn, 'The Migrations and other Habits of the Herring on the Coast of Devon and Cornwall', *Report of the Royal Cornwall Polytechnic Society*, 62 (1894), 58-72.

4 M. Dunn, 'Some Habits of the Picked Dogs, Herrings and Pilchards on the Coasts of Devon and Cornwall', *Report of the Royal Cornwall Polytechnic Society*, 54 (1886), 1-16.

5 J. T. Cunningham, 'Studies on the Reproduction and Development of Teleostan Fishes occurring in the Neighbourhood of Plymouth', *Journal of the Marine Biological Association of the United Kingdom* (hereafter *JMBA*), new series, 1 (1889), 10-54; 'The Reproduction and Growth of the Pilchard', *JMBA*, new series, 2 (1891), 151-7; 'The Life-History of the Pilchard' *JMBA*, new series, 3 (1894), 148-53.

6 J. C. A. Whetter, *The Economic History of Cornwall in the Seventeenth Century* (Padstow, 1974); M Culley, *The Pilchard: Biology and Exploitation* (Oxford, 1971).

7 J. T. Cunningham, 'Fishes', in W. Page, ed., *Victoria County History of Cornwall*, I, (1906), 291-306.

8 There were several different methods of salting herrings. See J. S. Dodd, *An Essay towards the Natural History of the Herring* (London, 1752).

9 J. Norden, *Speculi Britanniae Pars: A Topographical and Historical Description of Cornwall* (1728).

10 Past and recent methods of catching and preserving pilchards are summarized by Culley, *The Pilchard*. Further details are provided in J. Couch, 'A Treatise on the Natural History of the Pilchard, with particular reference to the Fisheries of Cornwall', *Report of the Royal Cornwall Polytechnic Society*, 3 (1835), 65-101, and J. Couch, *A History of the Fishes of the British Isles*, IV, (1865).

11 See R. H. Tawney and E. Power, *Tudor Economic Documents*, 2 vols, (1924); A. L. Rowse, *Tudor Cornwall* (1941), and *The England of Elizabeth* (1950).

12 See Tawney and Power, *Tudor Economic Documents*; J. Couch, 'Observations in Further Illustration of the History and Statistics of the Pilchard Fishery', *Transactions of the Polytechnic Society of Cornwall*, (1840), 11-26; R. N. Worth, *A History of Plymouth* (Plymouth, 1890); A. L. Rowse, 'The Dispute concerning the Plymouth Pilchard Fishery', *Economic History Review*, 1st series, II (1932), 461-5.

13 Couch, 'Observations...of the Pilchard Fishery'.

14 Norden, *Speculi Britanniae Pars*.

15 Whetter, *Economic History of Cornwall*.

16 We are indebted to Alison Grant for this information.

17 Whetter, *Economic History of Cornwall*.

18 Defoe's 1724 comment is quoted by R. P. Chope, *Early Tours in Devon and Cornwall* (Exeter, 1918), 145-78.

19 For instance, see Pococke's comments of 1750, and those of Shaw expressed in 1788; both are quoted in Chope, *Early Tours*, 178-215, 215-33.

20 R. Polwhele, *Devonshire*, I, (Exeter, 1797).

21 J. C. Bellamy, *The Natural History of South Devon* (Plymouth, 1839).

22 Quoted in Chope, *Early Tours*, 233-78.

23 Polwhele, *Devonshire*; D. Lysons & S. Lysons, *Magna Brittania, VI, Devonshire* (1822); E.A.S. Elliot, 'An Original Article by Colonel Montagu on the Pilchard Fishery at Borrough Island a hundred years ago: with Supplementary Notes to the Present Time', *Transactions of the Devonshire Association*, 35 (1903), 430-3.

24 J.C. Bellamy, *The Housekeeper's Guide to the Fishmarket for Each Month of the Year: And an Account of the Fisheries of Devon and Cornwall* (Plymouth, 1843).

25 *Report of the Commissioners appointed to Inquire into the Sea Fisheries of the United Kingdom*, II, evidence of W.F. Collier, (HMSO, 1865), 409.

26 *Report... Sea Fisheries*, II, evidence of M. Dunn and J. Easton, 418-9.

27 *Report... Sea Fisheries*, II, evidence of J. Easton and Captain Hawker, RN, 416-9.

28 Somerset County Record Office, Taunton, *Pulmans Weekly News*, 1857-85.

29 J. Couch, 'Some Particulars of the Natural History of Fishes found in Cornwall', *Transactions of the Linnear Society of London*, 14 (1822), 69-92.

30 *Report... Sea Fisheries*, II, evidence of J Couch, 466-72.

31 Quoted in Chope, *Early Tours*, 233-78.

32 Bellamy, *Housekeeper's Guide*.

33 Bellamy, *Housekeeper's Guide*; see W Roach, 'Notes on the Herring, Longline and Pilchard Fisheries of Plymouth during the Winter 1889-90', *JMBA*, new series, I (1890), 382-90; and 'Notes on the Herring, Longline, and Pilchard Fisheries of Plymouth (continued)', *JMBA*, new series, 2 (1891), 180-8; W. Heape, 'Notes on the Fishing Industry of Plymouth', *JMBA*, old series, 1 (1887), 45-95.

34 Dunn, 'Some Habits of the Picked Dogs'.

35 Couch, *History of the Fishes; Report... Sea Fisheries*, II, evidence of J. Couch.

36 M. Dunn, 'The Migrations and Habits of the Pilchard', in *Lectures on Fishes, Fishing etc, delivered at the Fisheries Exhibition, Truro, 1893* (Truro, 1895).

37 E.S. Russell, 'Report on Log-book Records relating to Mackerel, Pilchards, and Herring, kept by Fishermen during the years 1895-1911, under the auspices of Cornwall County Council', *Fishery Investigations, Series 2*, 3 pt 1 (1915), 1-46.

38 D.H. Cushing, 'On the Failure of the Plymouth Herring Fishery', *JMBA*, 41 (1961), 799-816.

39 Recollections of D. Taylor and G. Boalch.

40 D.H. Cushing, 'The Number of Pilchards in the Channel', *Fishery Investigations, Series 2*, 21 pt 5 (1957), 1-27; A.J. Southward, 'The Distribution of some Plankton Animals in the English Channel and Approaches: III. Theories about Long-term Biological Changes, including Fish', *JMBA*, 43 (1963), 1-27.

41 S. Kemp, 'Oceanography and the Fluctuations in Abundance of Marine Animals', *Report of the British Association for the Advancement of Science*, (1938), 85-101; L.H.N. Cooper, 'Deep-water Movements in the North Atlantic as a link between Climatic Changes around Iceland and Biological Productivity of the English Channel and Celtic Sea', *Journal of Marine Research*, 14 (1955), 347-62.

42 Recent evidence suggests that there were two spawning periods for pilchard, involving different fish, with a slight difference in egg size. See A.J. Southward and N. Demir, 'The Abundance and Distribution of Eggs and Larvae of Teleost Fishes off Plymouth in 1969 and 1970. Part 3. Eggs of Pilchard (*Sardinia pilchards* Walbaum) and Sprat (*Sprattus sprattus (L.)*', *JMBA*, 54 (1974), 333-53.

43 Cunningham, 'Fishes'.

44 Cushing, 'Number of Pilchards' and 'Failure of Plymouth Herring Fishery'; A.J. Southward, 'Long-term Changes in Abundance of Eggs of the Cornish Pilchard (*Sardinia pilchardus* Walbaum) off Plymouth', *JMBA*, 54 (1974), 641-9.

45 G. Manley, 'Central England Temperatures: Monthly Means from 1659 to 1973', *Quarterly Journal of the Royal Meterological Society*, 100 (1974), 389-405; H.H. Lamb, *Climate: Present, Past and Future*, II, *Climatic History and the Future* (1977).

46 See R.H. Dicke, 'Solar Luminosity and the Sunspot Cycle', *Nature*, 280 (1979), 24-7; J. Gribbin, 'Geomagnetism and Climate', *New Scientist*, 89 (1981), 350-3; J. Gribbin, 'Sun and Weather: the Stratospheric Link',

New Scientist, 91 (1981), 669-71; A. Long, '100 to 200 year Solar Periodicities', *Nature*, 298 (1982), 223; D. Gough, 'What causes the Solar Cycle?', *Nature*, 319 (1986), 263-4.

47 M. Waldmeier, *The Sunspot Activity in the years 1610-1960* (Zurich, 1961); M. Waldmeier, 'The Sunspot Activity in the years 1961-1975', *Astronomische Mitteilungen, Zurich*, 346 (1976), 1-13.

48 J.A. Eddy, 'The Maunder Minimum', *Science*, 192 (1976), 1189- 1202; M. Stuiver and P.D. Quay, 'Changes in Atmospheric Carbon-14 attributed to a Variable Sun', *Science*, 207 (1980), 11-19.

49 For instance, see E.J. Allen, 'Mackerel and Sunshine', *JMBA*, 8 (1910), 394-406; I.B. Birman, 'Heliohydrobiological Relations as a Basis for the Long-term Forecasting of Food Fish Stocks (with special reference to salmon and herring)', *Journal of Ichthyology*, 13 pt. 1 (1973), 20-32; O. Moura and G. Afonso dos Santos, 'Relating Pilchard Abundance to Solar Activity', Paper delivered at the meeting of the International Council for the Exploration of the Sea, 1984, paper H:48.

50 Cushing, 'Failure of Plymouth Herring Fishery'.

51 Southward, 'Distribution of some Plankton Animals'.

52 A.J. Southward, C.I. Butler, and L. Pennycuick, 'Recent Cyclic Changes in Climate and in Abundance of Marine Life', *Nature*, 253 (1975), 714-7.

53 A.J. Southward, 'The Western English Channel – an Inconstant Ecosystem?', *Nature*, 285 (1980), 361-6.

54 M. Dunn, 'On the Occurrence of Large Numbers of Larval Herrings at the Surface', *JMBA*, 5 (1898), 184-5.

55 M. Dunn, 'Migrations and Other Habits', and 'Some Habits of the Picked Dogs'.

56 J. Radovich, 'The Collapse of the California Sardine Fishery. What have we Learned?', in M.H. Glantz and J.D. Thompson, eds, *Resource Management and Environmental Uncertainty* (New York, 1981), 107-36.

57 J. Hansen *et al*, 'Climatic Impact of Increasing Atmospheric Carbon Dioxide', *Science*, 213 (1981), 957-66.

HANDLING THE 'FULLY-RIGGED SHIP'

Peter Allington

Introduction

The introduction of steam power revolutionized the shipping industry in the nineteenth century. This new form of propulsion was developed in the early years of this period but it was not until the 1880s that the advent of the triple-expansion compound engine gave steamers a decisive competitive edge over sailing vessels in the trans-oceanic trades. Until this time, wind-powered vessels continued to play a considerable part in international trade, their efficiency being enhanced by technological advances such as the use of iron, and later steel, in hull construction. Indeed, in areas such as south-west England the maritime communities, for a variety of reasons, never really adopted steam propulsion, and sailing vessels remained important to the economies of these regions into the present century. The problems of handling such vessels is therefore pertinent, for the successful negotiation of fundamental factors like wind, tide and current had a direct bearing on the efficiency of commercial operations. Accordingly, this paper deals with 'shiphandling' as it applied to trading vessels under sail, concentrating upon three aspects: firstly, the physical characteristics of vessel and wind which faced the sailing shipmaster; secondly, the theoretical principles underlying sailing ship operation; and, finally, a more detailed study of the handling of the least understood type of wind-powered craft, the three-masted 'fully-rigged ship'.

Physical constraints

With regard to the vessel propelled solely by the wind, 'shiphandling' may be defined as 'the art of manoeuvring the craft using the wind and tide, by control of her sails and rudder when underway'. Principally, this concerns changing the vessel's heading by 'tacking', or 'wearing', stopping her by 'heaving to', and getting underway; other considerations, such as the working of anchors, the various methods of moving her in a tideway and getting on and off a quay, and the management of the vessel in bad weather, ice, and other close-quarter situations, are also involved. Naturally, 'shiphandling' is constrained by the physical characteristics of the vessel – her size and rig – and the nature of the prime motive force, the wind.

Hull size

In terms of hull size, the nineteenth century witnessed major developments, creating particular handling problems, especially in confined waters. While the typical three-masted 'fully-rigged ship' of 1800 was wooden built, about 100 feet in length, the tall sail plan and large crew enabling her to work in harbours and up rivers, the equivalent vessel of the 1890s was over 250 feet in length, with a much larger area of canvas supported by steel masts and yards, a relatively small crew, and a carrying capacity of 3200 tons. These 'giants' were much less 'handy' than their predecessors, a disadvantage readily apparent when 'sea room' was at a premium, and overcome largely with the assistance of steam tugs in the major ports.

Rigging

A variety of rigs were employed in nineteenth-century vessels, though two main groups can be identified; thus, the 'square-rigged' vessel incorporated 'barques', 'barquentines', 'fully-rigged ships', 'brigs', and 'brigantines', while the 'fore-and-aft rigged' category included variants such as the 'cutter', 'ketch', 'schooner' (topsail and fore-and-aft), and 'sloop', together with the 'spritsail' rig typical of barges and river craft, and the 'lugsail' common in fishing vessels. The basic difference between the two classifications lay in the type of sail responsible for the bulk of motive force, 'square' or 'fore-and-aft'. This is an important factor in shiphandling, for in propelling the vessel forward, the wind is always striking the after side of a 'square' sail, whereas a 'fore-and-aft' sail can have the wind on either side, depending on the vessel's aspect relative to the eye of the wind. In general, the 'fore-and-aft' sail allowed the vessel to lie closer to the wind, pointing up to 45 degrees, or four points from the eye of the wind at best, when set over a well-shaped hull. On the other hand, when the 'Square Rigger' is sailing as close to the wind as possible, or 'close-hauled', she can only point up to approximately 70 degrees, or about six points, to the eye of the wind. If she tries to sail closer she is termed 'pinching' and the forward drive is much reduced as the square sails start to lift or flap.

The 'Square-Rigger', therefore, is less efficient than the 'fore-and-aft rigged' vessel when working to windward. This is of prime importance in waters such as the English Channel where winds are variable and land is in close proximity. Moreover, the figures given are for ideal conditions, and it should be noted that a light wind and heavy swell, or a gale and rough sea, will undoubtedly increase the angle relative to the wind. The loading and condition of the hull can also affect progress to windward; thus, a vessel in ballast, with her bottom covered in weed and barnacles, her course made good through the water, might be as much as 90 degrees or more relative to the wind. Safe anchorages were thus very important to vessels with poor windward ability trying to work up and down the English Channel. Devon is blessed with two of the finest on the south coast, Plymouth Sound and Torbay. The latter, in particular, with its wide approach, relatively free of danger, gives good shelter from the prevailing SW to NW winds. The bottom is clear of rocks and is mostly clay, giving particularly good holding to anchors. Should the wind be out of the east, Plymouth Sound affords good shelter.

Further inefficiencies are apparent in vessels sailing 'close hauled', for only a fraction of the wind's strength is converted into forward motion, while the most part acts to push her sideways. This is resisted by the underwater part of the hull, but some lateral movement is experienced. Such 'leeway' is at its maximum in light winds with the vessel 'close hauled', and zero when the wind is blowing directly from aft. It is usually expressed in terms of the angle between the vessel's heading and her true track through the water in degrees, though in the past it was referred to in points and quarter points. Many vessels have been lost purely because they could not get clear of a 'lee shore', and in the last resort anchors are the only means of salvation, the principal reason why sailing vessels carried such large ground tackle in relation to their size.

The Wind

The sailing ship, unlike the steam-driven vessel, can never control the source of her power, and is passively dependent upon the fickle, ever-changing wind, with the supplementary assistance of tides and ocean current. She was often forced to wait at anchor or delay her departure from harbour until conditions were favourable. Dartmouth, for example, with its narrow entrance and high land on both sides was particularly difficult for the 'Square Rigger', as the following advice in the *Seaman's Guide* of 1847 makes clear:

Ships coming from sea, and obliged to wait for an opportunity to enter, frequently anchor without the harbour, in what is called the Range, in from 5 to 6 fathoms. The wind from the SE to ESE blows true in, and from the NW to NE true out; all other winds blow in flaws.

In 1805, Francis Beaufort devised a scale for measuring wind speed, the gradations, measured at a height of 33 feet above sea level, range from 0 (calm) to force 12 (hurricane). The wind can also be expressed as a force or pressure measured in pounds per square foot for a given velocity, the force increasing in proportion to the square of the wind speed. In other words, if the wind's velocity doubles, the pressure quadruples; thus, force 5 on the Beaufort scale has a mean wind speed of 19 knots, exerting a pressure of 1.3 lbs per square foot on a surface at right angles to it, but at force 8, or 37 knots, the pressure increases to 5.3 lbs per square foot. A further measure of the wind's strength, and that most germane to the sailor on board ship, is the 'apparent' or 'relative' wind speed, a combination of the wind's true velocity and direction, and his ship's speed and course relative to it. Even in a flat calm, a vessel underway in a strong tidal flow would stimulate a light 'apparent' wind as she moved through still air. In a handy craft with a good rig and a clean bottom this was often sufficient to fill the lighter sails and give steerage way.

The implications of these characteristics of the wind for the handling of sailing ships can be illustrated by a hypothetical example. Thus, a three-masted 'fully-rigged ship', carrying square sails on all masts, is running before a gale at 10 knots with reduced canvas; with a true wind speed of 37 knots, the apparent wind to those on board would be about 27 knots from right astern; this would exert a pressure of 3 lbs per square foot on all surfaces exposed at right angles to it, and, making allowance for some of the wind escaping around the edges of the sail and fluctuations in the wind's strength and direction, roughly 1000 square foot of sail would develop 1 ton of forward thrust, while the exposed part of the hull and upperworks would also assist forward progress.

If for some reason, the same vessel, in similar conditions, was 'close hauled' with the yards braced sharp up and the sail area reduced, her speed would be much less, perhaps down to 4 knots with the ship now making leeway. To those aboard, the apparent wind speed has increased to 40 knots as she now heads toward the eye of the wind, albeit at an angle of 70 degrees, exerting a pressure of 6 lbs per square foot on the sails. However, as it strikes the sails at a fine angle only a fraction of this increased 'power' is converted into forward drive, the bulk of it pressing the vessel to leeward, all exposed surfaces now retarding progress.

Given such differing responses to wind velocity and direction, sudden shifts can be highly dangerous, not only close inshore with restricted 'sea room', but also in the open ocean. Vigilance is therefore required, for a ship might be caught under full sail, a vicious squall perhaps causing a breeze to increase to hurricane force in a few minutes, and, at the same time, altering wind direction by 180 degrees. Normally, there is some warning, and the upper sails can be taken in or furled, and the vessel made ready to run off before the squall as the safest course of action. If, however, she is caught 'aback', the squall striking the forward sides of her square sails, she might be blown over on her 'beam ends'. A shifting cargo is a further hazard in these situations, pinning the vessel down on her side, out of control with her rudder near horizontal and ineffective.

General Principles of Shiphandling

Point of balance

When the rudder is turned to one side by the action of the helm or steering gear, a vessel moving ahead through the water changes course, to some extent, like a car skidding on ice. Her bows may now be pointing in a different direction, but there is still a tendency for her to carry on bodily in the same track. The hull will slip sideways somewhat, depending on her draught, and she will rotate about a point a little way ahead of the mid-position. If she has sternway, the point about which she rotates when turning will move well aft of the mid-point. For all practical purposes, this can be considered her point of balance. Should the bows be depressed for some reason, her centre of gravity will move forward, as will her point of balance; conversely, the balance point will move aft on the depression of the stern. Due to the ship's motion and heel, this point is never constant, but its location can be gauged by the experienced shipmaster, and used to advantage.

Drifting

It is important to know how a vessel will drift, and what aspect relative to the wind she will adopt when under way with no sail set. This will vary according to her lading, trim and rig. The majority of sailing vessels, especially those with long bowsprits and a high forecastle head, will tend to have their bows blow off downwind in normal trim, and, thus, they drift bodily to leeward at an angle with the stern seeking the wind. Hence, even under bare poles, the vessel will gather way, and once a flow is established past the rudder she can be steered either diagonally or directly downwind, her speed dependent upon the strength of the wind.

Sail balance

The distribution of sail area fore and aft of the 'balance point' is the basis of the management of a vessel under canvas. In a ship sailing with the wind on her beam, the area ahead of the balance point will tend to turn her bows away from the wind, while sail set aft of this position will tend to do the opposite. It follows that, area for area, those sails furthest from the point of balance, due to their longer 'lever arm', will exert the greatest turning effect.

In general, a vessel should have her sails set and trimmed so that she can steer the desired course with minimum use of the rudder. This is more easily achieved with the wind forward of the beam, for once the relative wind is well out on the quarter some of the sails in the middle and, especially in the forepart of the vessel, will be masked by those aft, thereby destroying the balance. In such instances, the necessary remedy is the reduction of sail aft, or the easing of sheets on those sails so as to spill some wind. Perfect sail balance is not attempted with the wind on the bow round to a couple of points abaft the beam. A slight preponderance of sail aft of the balance point results in a small amount of 'weather helm' being required to counteract the tendency of the vessel to come up into the wind. This affords 'feel' to the steering, allowing the maintenance of a better course; it is also safer, in most cases, should anything go wrong with the rudder, for the vessel will then round up into the wind so that her square sails are aback, and she will therefore stop.

To alter course, particularly in a hurry, the sails should be worked in conjunction with the rudder, being retrimmed or taken in as appropriate. In normal circumstances she would be 'sailed' round, using only as much rudder angle as required to maintain the swing. Thus, if a ship sailing 'close hauled' finds it necessary to turn away from the wind the helm is put 'up', or 'a weather'. Sail pressure aft of the balance point is then reduced by easing off the sheets, or taking in sail. In a three-masted 'fully-rigged ship', the square sails on the aftermost mast, the mizzen, would be 'shivered', the yards being braced round so that they are virtually pointing at the wind, reducing not only the forward drive, but also, significantly, neutralizing their turning effect. With all her sail set ahead of the balance point, the vessel rapidly turns away from the wind.

To turn her towards the wind, or 'come up', the sail 'leverage' aft of the balance point should be increased, and that forward of it decreased. In the three-masted 'fully-rigged ship', the 'spanker', or gaff sail on the mizzen, is hauled amidships, and the helm 'put down' or to leeward. Leverage forward of the balance point should then be reduced, the most effective way being to ease up on the jib sheets, or to drop these sails temporarily down their stays. If this action proves insufficient, a further reduction in sail pressure forward might be effected by 'shivering' the square sail on the foremast, bracing the yards round so as to nearly point at the wind.

Stability

Stability in the sailing ship is vital. Lacking it, the 'crank' vessel is forced to reduce sail and lose speed every time the breeze picks up, lest she be blown over. A number of factors might cause, or contribute to, this condition. Firstly, it might result from the poor stowage of cargo, with heavy weights at the top of the hold, or on deck, raising the centre of gravity. Secondly, the carriage of a very light cargo with insufficient ballast might lead to instability. In fact, the vast majority of ocean-going sailing vessels required some ballast – usually pig iron, stones, gravel, or sand – when carrying light loads or no cargo at all. The amount required varied with each vessel, and depended upon the passage to be taken and the time of the year. If, for example, she was to change berths in the same port after the discharge of her cargo, the minimum amount would be used, sufficient to prevent her from falling over. On the other hand, an outward bound winter voyage around Cape Horn would require considerably more ballast, well secured against shifting.

The third factor leading to 'crank' vessels is the relation of hull shape to the height of the rig and amount of 'top hamper'. Hull form, or more particularly the shape of the midship cross section of a vessel, and its beam to length ratio, has a direct bearing on her initial stability. It is self evident that a broad plank of wood is more stable when floating than one with a square cross-section. If, instead, the shape were an equilateral triangle, then weight must be added to one corner to prevent it from rolling over. Therefore, the vessel with more beam than depth is inherently more stable; yet, for a given draught it presents virtually a maximum of wetted surface area and hence drag, while the triangular section, which offers the least drag, would be the faster hull, but would require ballast to remain upright. Waterline length is also significant in respect of speed, for a long, narrow hull is potentially faster than a short, beamy one of the same displacement. In reality, this conflict between carrying capacity and speed has produced two extremes; while barges provide the greatest initial stability and carrying capacity, clipper ships, with a high beam to length ratio, possess more of a triangular-shaped midship section with fine ends, rendering them fast, but with stowage of cargo difficult, and much ballast essential.

Vessels that carry a great deal of sail without laying over on their sides, even in a fresh breeze, are termed 'stiff'. This condition can be dangerous, for 'stiffness' results in a short, sharp roll, with dismasting a possibility due to the violent motion in a heavy swell with no wind. This problem is often caused by the carriage of particularly heavy cargoes, such as iron or copper ore stowed low down. One solution is to raise the vessel's centre of gravity by constructing a strong platform in the hold above the keel.

Thus, various physical factors affect the handling of wooden sailing vessels. However, one crucial variable has yet to be mentioned – the crew. In many situations, a skilled and confident master, with a strong, experienced crew, might execute manoeuvres which a less able complement would not even attempt.

Handling the three-masted 'fully-rigged ship'

The three-masted 'fully-rigged ship' exhibited the classic sail plan – illustrated in Figure 1 – which dominated the trade routes from the early seventeenth century to the last days of deep-water commercial sail. Slowly developed and modified throughout this period, reaching a peak in terms of speed with the clipper ships, it was commonly employed in men-of-war and trans-oceanic traders. This three-masted rig was utilised in some of the large steel-hulled sailing vessels of the late nineteenth century, though with the growth in hull size one or even two additional masts were required to spread the sail plan without increasing the size of the individual sails.

To appreciate the techniques used to handle the three-masted 'fully-rigged ship', five basic manoeuvres have been identified and will be discussed independently. Two of the manoeuvres concern the methods by which the 'Square-Rigger' left, and came to, an anchorage, while the other three concern the principal means of changing the vessel's tack at sea – 'tacking', 'wearing', and 'boxhauling'.

A Sailing from an anchorage

The vessel is prepared for sea; her hatches are battened down, boats swung inboard, gangway unshipped, and pilot ladder rigged if necessary. The steering gear is tested, the yards are braced, and such sail as required for getting underway is made ready for hoisting or sheeting home. Much depends upon the situation of the wind and the tide, the proximity of other vessels, and navigation hazards; moreover, the handling characteristics of the vessel are further significant variables – how quickly she gathers way, and how responsive she is to her sails and helm. Nevertheless, two general rules apply to the 'Square-Rigger'. Firstly, the ship's head must be cast away from the riding anchor so that the latter is on the weather bow when retrieved by the 'cat' and 'fish' tackles. Secondly, the ship's head should be cast towards the nearest hazard as she will make a sternboard as soon as the anchor is aweigh, thereby backing away from the obstruction, which eventually appears on the weather bow. This is in direct contrast to the 'fore-and-aft' rigged vessel which is cast away from the hazard so that the initial tack propels her further away from it as she gathers headway.

In Figure 2, the three masted 'fully-rigged ship' has single topsails, and is laying to her port anchor. She is in a moderate breeze, with no tidal flow, or dangers close at hand, and she is ready to get underway on the port tack.

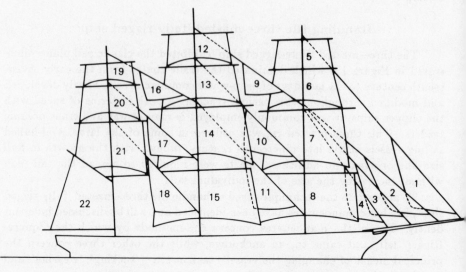

1 Flying Jib	12 Main Royal
2 Outer Jib	13 Main Topgallant
3 Inner Jib	14 Main Topsail
4 Fore Topmast Staysail	15 Mainsail (Maincourse)
5 Fore Royal	16 Mizzen Royal Staysail
6 Fore Topgallant	17 Mizzen Topgallant Staysail
7 Fore Topsail	18 Mizzen Topmast Staysail
8 Foresail (Forecourse)	19 Mizzen Royal
9 Main Royal Staysail	20 Mizzen Topgallant
10 Main Topgallant Staysail	21 Mizzen Topsail
11 Main Topmast Staysail	22 Spanker

Figure 1
Sail Plan of the Three Masted 'Fully-Rigged Ship'

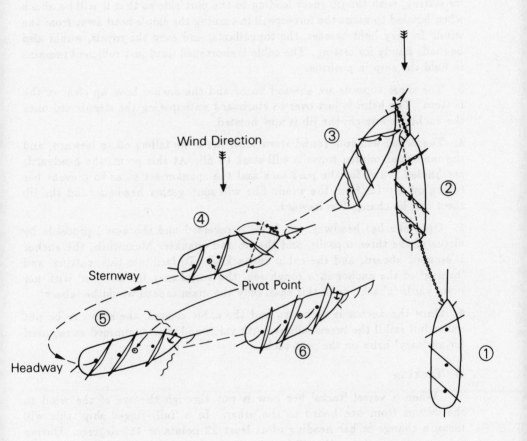

Figure 2
Sailing from an Anchorage

1. The 'cat' and 'fish' tackles are rigged over the port bow in readiness, and the capstan bars shipped. The headyards are braced 'a-box', for the starboard tack, so that the sails on the foremast, being aback, will send the bows away to starboard. The yards on the main and mizzen masts are braced the other way, for the intended port tack.

2. The sail required initially – usually the three single topsails – is loosed from its gaskets and hangs ready in its gear. The jib and spanker are prepared for setting, with the jib sheet leading to the port side so that it will be aback when hoisted to assist the foretopsail in turning the ship's head away from the wind. In very light breezes, the topgallants, and even the royals, would also be made handy for setting. The cable is shortened until just sufficient remains to hold the ship in position.

3. The three topsails are sheeted home and the anchor hove up clear of the bottom. The helm is just over to starboard anticipating the sternboard once the anchor is aweigh; the jib is now hoisted.

4. The vessel will spin round stern first, the bows falling off to leeward, and the main and mizzen topsails will start to fill. At this point, the headyards are hauled round for the port tack and the spanker set so as to prevent her falling off too far from the wind. She will soon gather headway, and the jib sheet can be changed to leeward.

5. Once she has headway, the helm is reversed and the vessel proceeds by virtue of the three topsails, and the jib and spanker. Meanwhile, the anchor is secured aboard, and the cable unshackled. To facilitate this 'catting' and 'fishing' of the anchor in a rough sea, the vessel may be 'hove to' with her main yards 'aback', or in this case, only the main topsail would be 'aback'.

6. Once the anchor is on board and the cable cleared, the ship can be put under full sail if the breeze allows, with yards and sheets trimmed as required for an 'easy' helm on the port tack.

B Tacking

When a vessel 'tacks' her bow is put through the eye of the wind as she swings from one board to the other. In a 'fully-rigged ship' this will mean a change in her heading of at least 12 points or 135 degrees. During this manoeuvre, her sails will lose forward drive at one point, and hence she requires a certain momentum to accomplish it successfuly. 'Tacking' is thus difficult in light winds, particularly if there is a swell. Conversely, in very strong winds, even under reduced canvas, it is a potentially dangerous manoeuvre for damage may occur to the ship's sails and gear. The rapid swing to windward, combined with heavy pitching in a rough sea, with square sails 'aback', exerts a tremendous strain on the relatively few fore and aft stays supporting the masts.

Though each vessel displays its own handling characteristics, rendering generalisations difficult, it will be assumed in the following outline – illustrated in Figure 3 – that the vessel's trim, draft, and rig, together with the

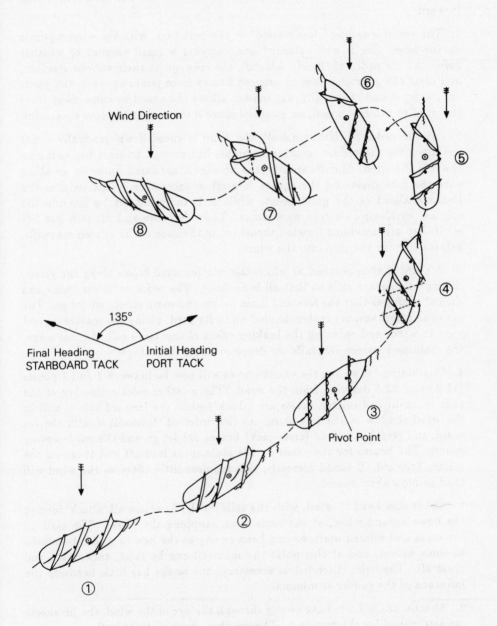

Wind Direction

135°

Final Heading
STARBOARD TACK

Initial Heading
PORT TACK

Pivot Point

① ② ③ ④ ⑤ ⑥ ⑦ ⑧

Figure 3
Tacking

condition of the wind and sea, are all conducive to 'tacking' the ship. However, a consideration applying to all vessels is that ground will be gained to windward in the process of 'tacking', a vital factor if there is little searoom to leeward.

1. The vessel is sailing 'close hauled' on the port tack, with the wind 6 points on the bow. She is well balanced and carrying a small amount of weather helm. At the order of 'Ready About!', the crew go to their various stations, and clear the gear and lines to prevent blocks from jamming when the yards are swung round. Generally, the master allows the vessel to come away from the wind to increase speed, an essential move if the tack is to prove successful.

2. At the order of 'Helms a lee!', the helm is eased down gradually – not too much for the rudder to act as a brake, but enough to start her swinging towards the wind. Simultaneously, the jib sheets are eased up or let go along with the fore sheets on the square foresail or forecourse. This reduces the leverage ahead of the pivot point, while it is increased aft by hauling the spanker amidships, or even to weather. The other fore and aft sails are left set if they are providing forward thrust or, in the case of the mizzen staysails, helping to turn the ship into the wind.

3. A point is soon reached at which the relative wind blows along the yards, 'lifting' the square sails so that all is shaking. The order of 'Raise tacks and sheets!' requires that the fore and main tacks, and main sheet, are let go. The mainsail (main course) is then hauled up to its yard, giving the master a good view forward, and reducing the braking effect of this large sail. At this stage, the main and mizzen staysails are dropped down their stays.

4. Continuing her swing, the vessel's bows will now be between 1 and 2 points (11.25 and 22.5 degrees) from the wind. The weather sides or leeches of the sails on main and mizzen masts are 'aback', while the leeward side is still in the wind shadow of the fore sails. At the order of 'Mainsail Haul!', the lee main, and weather mizzen (cross-jack) braces are let go and the yards swung round. The braces for the yards on the main mast lead aft and those on the mizzen forward. If timed correctly, this requires little effort as the wind will tend to blow them round.

5. She is now head to wind, with the sails on the foremast all 'aback' forcing the bows around while, at the same time, stopping the vessel. The sails on the main and mizzen mast, having been swung to the new tack, are becalmed to some extent, and at this point the mainsail can be reset, tack down and sheet aft. The helm is tended as necessary, but as she has little headway the influence of the rudder is minimal.

6. As soon as the bows have swung through the eye of the wind, the jib sheets are retrimmed for the new tack. The spanker sheet is slacked off.

7. When she is round sufficiently for the sails on the main and mizzen masts to fill, and there is no longer any possibility of her reversing the swing, the order 'Let go and haul!' is given. The yards on the foremast are then braced

around as quickly as possible, and the foresail (forecourse) tacked down on the new weather side and the sheet led aft. Before she loses all headway, the helm is put over to the new leeward side to prevent the bows from swinging too far. To assist in this, the spanker might be sheeted amidships once more, the jib sheets can be eased, or the fore yards swung not right around, but trimmed so that the sails are shaking as the yards lie parallel to the wind. Naturally, this will reduce the leverage forward of the pivot point. If, on the other hand, she has a strong tendency to fly up into the wind, the sail pressure will have to be reduced aft by brailing in the spanker or 'shivering' the mizzen yards.

8. Once she has settled down on the new tack the staysails can be re-set and all the braces and sheets trimmed for the new heading. All the gear is coiled neatly and secured. The extra crew required to tack the ship can now 'stand down'.

C Wearing

'Wearing' is the opposite to 'tacking' in that the vessel is turned away from the wind, running before it at one stage, with the swing continued until she is once more 'close hauled' on the new tack. This involves a change of heading of approximately 20 points or 225 degrees. Ground is lost to leeward in this manoeuvre, a fact which makes 'tacking' preferable. However, 'wearing' may be the only option for a master in certain conditions – either in light winds with the ship making insufficient headway, or in strong to gale force winds when the conditions are too dangerous for 'tacking', or in circumstances where the vessel is under manned.

'Wearing' generally takes longer than 'tacking', and clearly needs searoom to leeward. However, it can be accomplished with a much smaller crew, for speed is not required and, indeed, it is a manoeuvre best carried out with as little headway as possible, sufficient only for the vessel to respond to her helm. Moreover, at no point in 'wearing' a ship is the timing as critical as in 'tacking' when the orders 'Mainsail haul!' and 'Let go and haul!' have to be undertaken at the precise moment if the swing is to be maintained. Nevertheless, good judgement is required in 'wearing' a ship round in bad weather, as twice in the manoeuvre she is broadside onto the sea, critical junctures which must be timed to coincide with a lull in the wind or a gap in the large breaking waves.

In Figure 4 it is assumed that the winds are light and the ship is carrying full sail; she is well balanced, with a small amount of weather helm, and 'close hauled' on the port tack.

1. At the order 'Stand by to wear ship!', the hands proceed to their stations and clear the gear and lines in preparation for taking in sail and swinging the yards.

2. The 'spanker' is brailed in, the main and mizzen staysails are lowered down their stays and the mainsail tack and sheet are let go, and the sail is hauled up to the yard. The mainsail is taken in at this stage to reduce speed and, significantly, to allow a free flow of air to the fore sails once the wind draws aft.

71

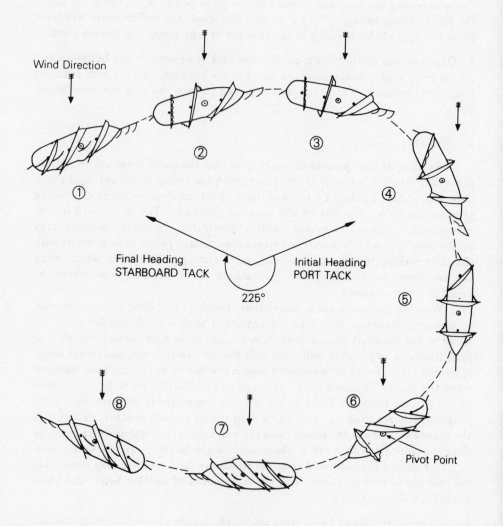

Wind Direction

① ② ③ ④ ⑤ ⑥ ⑦ ⑧

Final Heading
STARBOARD TACK

Initial Heading
PORT TACK

225°

Pivot Point

Figure 4
Wearing Ship

To further reduce sail pressure aft of the pivot point the yards on the mizzen mast are trimmed so that they are virtually pointing at the wind; the sails are now 'shaking', with no forward drive, and their turning effect is neutralised.

3. On the order 'Up helm!', the helm is put 'up', or to windward; due to the rudder's action, and the sail pressure forward of the pivot point provided by the jibs and forerails, the ship's head will pay off down wind. If she is travelling too fast the yards on the mainmast can be braced in, like those on the mizzen, so that the mainsails are 'shaking'.

4. The yards on the foremast are kept braced as near to right angles to the wind as possible. Those on the mainmast are treated in the same manner, unless there is a need for reducing speed, when they are trimmed to minimise the forward drive.

5. When the ship is before the wind the foresail (fore course) tack and sheet are let go and the sail hauled up to the yard. The jibs are lowered down the stays, as they might hinder the ship as she comes up to the new heading.

6. As she brings the wind on the other quarter, the yards on the main and mizzen masts are braced 'sharp up' for the new tack, the mainsail is re-set, and the spanker hauled out again, the sail being sheeted amidships.

7. The swing continues, and the headyards braced up for the next board, while the foresail is re-set and the jibs hoisted and trimmed to restore balance. The helm is now 'reversed' so as to 'meet her', or steady her up on the new tack. At this point, the main and mizzen staysails can be re-set and trimmed.

8. Once settled on the starboard tack, the yards and sails are trimmed to best advantage, the ship being well balanced with a slight 'weather helm'.

D Boxhauling

'Boxhauling' is a means of changing the ship from one tack to the other in confined waters, combining elements of 'tacking' in the first part of the manoeuvre, and 'wearing' in the latter stages. Initially, the vessel is stopped short by being brought nearly head to wind with the braces eased off on all the masts. She then gathers sternway, her foreyards braced at right angles to the wind, or 'boxed'. Finally, she forges ahead again as the wind comes aft, 'wearing' round on to the new tack. Having 'box-hauled', the ship will be on her new heading, though she will be in approximately her starting position. 'Boxhauling' normally takes much longer than either 'tacking' or 'wearing', but can be used to advantage if a vessel fails to tack, and her bows fall away from the wind onto her original heading.

In Figure 5, the ship is well balanced, and 'close hauled' in the port tack, with a small amount of weather helm.

1. On the order 'Standby to boxhaul!', the crew proceed to their stations, and the gear and lines are cleared for running.

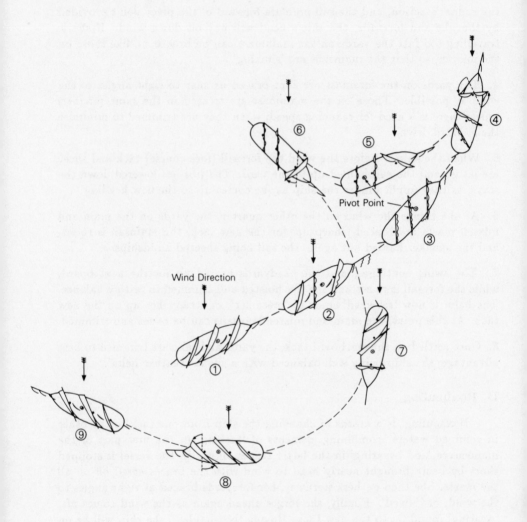

Pivot Point

Wind Direction

Figure 5
Boxhauling

2. To decrease the leverage forward, jibs and headsail sheets are eased up together with the foresheet, while the spanker is hauled amidships to increase its turning effect. As in 'tacking', the order of 'Helm's a lee' eases the helm down, though in 'boxhauling' more helm is given to bring the ship virtually head to wind in the shortest distance. This braking effect can be assisted by 'shaking' the sails on the mainmast by squaring in the yards.

3. As soon as the mainsail starts to lift, the command of 'Raise tacks and sheets!' is given, and the sail is hauled up to the yard. The foresail tack can be released, spanker brailed up, and the main and mizzen staysails lowered. So long as she is still swinging up to windward the forward drive of her sails should be reduced as much as possible.

4. Just before the ship is head to wind and almost stopped, the order 'Let go and haul!' – not 'Mainsail haul!' as in 'tacking' – is given. The fore-yards are then braced round so that they are at right angles to the wind, or 'boxed'. She will then come to a standstill, and the jib and headsail sheets can be flattened in.

5. The 'boxed' foresails push the vessel astern and swing the bows back on to the original heading. The rudder is left in its 'Helm's a lee' position, and the after square sails are kept lifting by pointing the yards at the wind so as not to impede her sternway. As she now has sternway and the pivot point has moved well aft, the leverage exerted by the foresails and headsails will be considerable, and consequently, she will rotate her stern very rapidly towards the wind.

6. The wind is soon abaft the beam, or on the quarter, and the fore-yards are squared. The vessel will therefore stop before beginning to gather headway once more.

7. The helm is now put a-weather, and once the wind has been brought round to the other quarter, the jibs and headsails are dropped. The spanker is hauled out, the mainsail re-set, and the main and mizzen yards braced 'sharp up' for the new tack.

8. As she comes up to the wind the fore-yards are braced up for the starboard tack, the foresail is tacked down and sheeted aft, and the jibs and headsails re-set. Once more, the pivot point has moved forward. The helm is tended as required, perhaps put 'a weather' to prevent the bows from swinging too close to the wind while the jibs are re-set.

9. Once settled on the new heading, the main and mizzen staysails can be hauled up and re-trimmed, while the braces, tacks, and sheets are given a final adjustment to leave the ship well balanced on the starboard tack.

E Coming to anchor

The sailing shipmaster was faced with a wide variety of wind and tidal conditions which determined his approach to the anchorage, as well as the amount of sail his ship was carrying. In a tideway, it is the motion over the sea bed that has to be taken into consideration, not just the ships' motion through the water. In most cases, the vessel would be 'rounded up' to wind or tide, whichever was the dominant factor, using her sails to best advantage, developing sternway before dropping the anchor. The cable would then be laid out on the bottom clear of the anchor. However, a ship running into an anchorage with a light, fair wind and the tide against her would not have to 'round up', but reduce sail until she was no longer travelling forward over the ground, letting go her anchor as she started to move 'backwards'. In a strong tide she would still have a bow wave and would appear to be forging ahead, but in relation to her anchor she would be moving away from it stern first.

The amount of cable required also depended on such factors as the nature of the bottom, the exposure of the anchorage, weather conditions, and the tidal strength. Normally, it was reckoned that the necessary length was three to four times the depth of water at high tide. With the old-fashioned windlass, the cable would be roused up on deck during the approach to the anchorage, and ranged to ensure that it ran cleanly once the anchor was released. As a precautionary measure, one of the ship's boats was made ready for lowering should it be required for running out a kedge anchor.

In Figure 6, the anchoring of a 'fully-rigged ship' is illustrated in its simplest form. She is equipped with the more modern type of windlass, the barrel or gypsy, over which the cable runs freely, controlled by a band brake. A fair breeze is blowing, and there is no tidal flow; the vessel is intending to lay to one anchor, and she is carrying single topsails.

1.   The port anchor is shackled on to its cable and put over the side, hanging from the cathead by the slip mechanism, the shank painter being made fast as well for security.

2.   Sail is taken in to reduce speed. Firstly, the royals and outer jibs are handed, followed by the top gallants, while the foresail is hauled up to its yard, clearing the for'castle head in readiness for letting go the anchor. The mainsail is taken up also, providing a clear view forward. Then the main staysails are handed, though, in some cases, a mizzen staysail, being aft of the pivot point, is left in place to help swing the ship's head to wind.

3.   The vessel's headway is much reduced as she approaches the anchoring ground. The foretopsail is now clewed up, leaving the ship under main and mizzen topsails, spanker, and one headsail or jib, and perhaps one mizzen staysail.

4.   To further reduce sail pressure ahead of the pivot point, the jib is handed and the main topsail clewed up if necessary. 'Helm's a lee!' – the helm is eased down and this, together with the spanker which is sheeted amidships or to weather, swings the ship's head to wind. At this point, the shank painter is released leaving the anchor cockbilled, being retained only by the slip mechanism on the cathead.

5.   The vessel is now head to wind with mizzen and, perhaps main topsail,

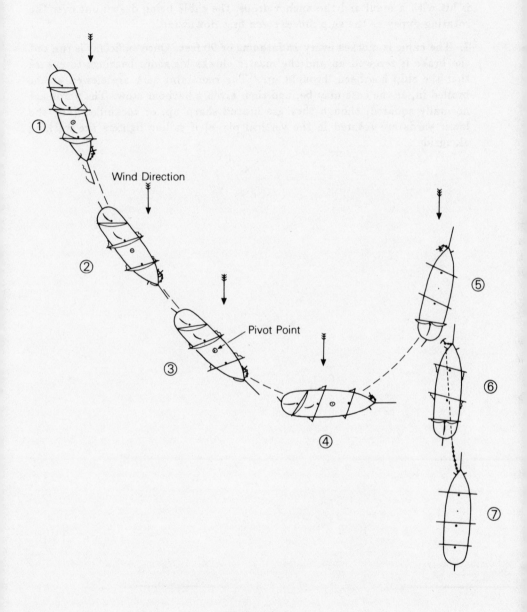

Wind Direction

Pivot Point

Figure 6
Coming to Anchor

aback and braced square to the ship. The spanker is sheeted flat amidships, and the mizzen staysail can be handed, if not done previously.

6. As she gathers sternway, the order of 'Let go!' is given; the release pin is hit with a maul and the anchor drops, the cable being drawn out over the rotating gypsy as the ship moves stern first downwind.

7. The cable is marked every 15 fathoms or 90 feet. Once sufficient is run out the brake is screwed up and the master checks his shore bearings to ensure that the ship has been 'brought up'. The remaining sails are clewed up, or brailed in, as the case may be, and then given a harbour stow. The yards are normally squared, though they are braced sharp up, or cockbilled (i.e. the lower yards are rotated in the vertical plane) if sailing lighters are working alongside.

SHIPHANDLING IN RESTRICTED WATERS

Edmund Eglinton

Introduction

Edmund Eglinton was a professional seaman from North Somerset who sailed in the 1920s in trows, ketches and schooners in the trade of the Bristol Channel, in the Irish trade, and in the general home trade. A number of the vessels he sailed in were owned in, or manned from, North Devon. He left the sea during the great depression of the late 1920s and worked as a labourer on a building site. Prospering, he was able in due course to retire back to North Somerset as a successful builder and property owner. In his late 70s and early 80s, at my suggestion, he wrote an account of his life at sea which was published as a book under the title of *The Last of the Sailing Coasters*. Beautifully written, the book was highly praised in *The Times Literary Supplement* and was most successful. After it was published, Edmund Eglinton prepared a second manuscript describing every detail of the life on board an imaginary North Devon ketch from Appledore which he called the *Mary Fletcher*. He found it easier to present the facts against a fictional background than to describe them in a purely documentary work. The result was perhaps the best account of the handling and management, and of the social relations of the crew, of a sailing vessel in the home trade ever to have been written. The manuscript is full of historical detail of the operation of craft skills now totally lost, and of social patterns which have long vanished. The extract which follows describes shiphandling in restricted tidal waters in the upper Bristol Channel.

Basil Greenhill

"The next day the captain returned from the ship broker's office with the news that he had been offered a cargo of coal from Newport to the river Yeo.

'I didn't give an answer straight away, George', he told the mate, 'I've never been there; thought I'd have a word with you first. I've heard you talk of it.'

'I was born not far from the pier', said George, 'but I can't understand them offering you a cargo. The only vessels that ever traded into that river are the two owned by the railway company – the *Sarah* and the *Lily*, and I've sailed in both.'

'What about depth of water, George? What did the *Sarah* draw?'

'She drew about ten feet, but you needn't worry, there's plenty of water for us. Easy enough to drop up the river with the anchor down should the wind be contrary', answered George.

'There's no soundings anywhere near the mouth of the river shown on my chart, is it all mudflats thereabouts?'

'Cap'n', said George, 'there's nought to worry about at all. When I joined the *Sarah* she had a new skipper who had never been into the Yeo. We had no trouble, I know every yard of those mudflats. My father and I stuck a sixteen-foot sapling on the best lead in over the bar. It had some twigs on the top, so we called it 'bushy stick'. It's probably still there; there's a cross bar nailed to it ten feet up.'

The captain, re-assured, made the short journey to the brokers and fixed for the cargo from Newport river to the Yeo, the crew to discharge the ship under the crane at the railway company's wharf on the west bank of the Yeo. The freightage was 2s 2d per ton, or 11 new pence, bringing the total freight for the *Mary Fletcher's* cargo of 130 tons to just over £14.

At slack tide the next morning just before high water (low water 11 pm, high water 6 am approx.) with all the mooring ropes aboard except a slip rope, they hoisted the head of the standing jib and, the wind being easterly, at dead high water that tiny bit of sail was sufficient, when the slip rope was hauled in, to blow the old ship with the 130 tons of coal in her hold off to mid-stream, where the anchor was let go ready to drop the ship astern downstream with the anchor acting as a drogue. This was the only way when the wind was foul to get to the river's mouth. But it was a simple and effective way.

It was nearly two miles to the mouth of the river, an hour and a half of anchor drill whilst the captain steered his ship stern first. Nevertheless, each man managed to enjoy a cold breakfast as they took turn about. Once clear of Fifoots Point the mainsail was set, the anchor hove clear of the bottom and, as she canted, two jibs were hauled up, the main sheet hauled hard in, next the mizzen was set, then the staysail. With the tide as it was running to windward at about four miles per hour, the *Mary Fletcher* was finding plenty of wind, but the mate suggested to Captain Trumper that if they wanted to get inside St Thomas's Head while there was plenty of water to accommodate the *Mary Fletcher's* eleven-foot draught it would be good policy to set the topsail. 'Otherwise', said George, 'we shall have to go below Sand Point and dodge about till the flood tide makes.'

Looking to the westward where the sky looked somewhat wild, Captain Trumper decided to take the mate's advice. Bending on the halyard and sheet, the two men hoisted the topsail aloft. The captain luffed his vessel into the eye of the wind to prevent the flogging topsail from filling, otherwise ten men could not have hauled it up, let alone two. The *Mary Fletcher* was really thrashing through the water now, her lee gunwale awash, and heavy spray flying aboard over her weather bow. Captain Trumper was finding it hard work to prevent her from luffing up, the vessel wanted so much weather helm. This meant she was not balanced; the answer would have been to set the flying jib, but that with the topsail set could have sprung the topmast. The obvious answer to that would have been to take in the topsail. Soon the vessel was clear of the West Middle Ground sand, with the English and Welsh Grounds lightship on her starboard's hand. She was finding the full force of the ebb now running out of the Severn sweeping her down to the west'ard, whilst the strong wind was lying her over to the east'ard; a state of affairs which, owing to the increasingly choppy sea and the resulting heavy spray, quickly disposed of any coal dust that may have been left in any non-accessible place in any part of the deck, or anywhere ten feet above. The dark green of Woodspring Hill could clearly be seen right ahead.

The mate, seeing the anxious glances Captain Trumper was casting aloft, told Arthur to cast off the coils of the topsail halyards and stand by ready to run the sail down if given the word. They were now well in over the English Grounds, and George could see the ridge of the Langford Sands, the tail of which they would soon have to pass. He was on familiar ground now and, as he expected, he could see the highest part of the ridge was on the western end. This, as he pointed out to the captain, was the result of such a long spell of easterly winds which they had experienced on the dreary passage over from the Irish coast.

'Captain,' said George – for he noticed the worried look on the captain's face – 'with this strong breeze we can afford to keep clear of the tail of the sand altogether, take her in to within a cable's length of the Head [St Thomas's]. The ebb's a bit strong in there but with the topsail set she'll run up over that.' Then he added, 'if she don't stem it, there's plenty of water astern of her in there!'

Arthur, looking out of his galley doorway on the windward side – where he was only two steps from the topsail halyards – called out to say he could see sheep on the hill. It was a huge flock, weaving about like an enormous blanket, obviously being rounded up by a dog.

Now they could see the dog. 'Time you took over, I think, George', said the captain, indicating the wheel. The mate found it needed all his weight to keep the ship from luffing up, but this was good, he knew she'd stem the little tide race they would encounter when rounding St Thomas's Head. Exhilarated at the thought of entering the old and isolated river he knew so well, in addition to the satisfaction of being proved right in his advice to the captain, he called to Arthur to stand by to ease off the main sheet.

Looking straight at Captain Trumper he said, 'Shall I stand by the mizzen sheet, captain?' The captain, sensing George's dilemma, that it may be imprudent to give an order to himself, said 'You stay where you are George, and don't be afraid to holler!'

The mate watching the changing scene ashore as the tide swept them to the westward, and glancing astern every few seconds where he could see the N.W. Elbow buoy, was waiting until St Thomas's Head, the ship, and the buoy were in one straight line, for then he knew they would be below the extreme tail of the Langford Grounds.

There they were, dead in line! 'Ease off the sheets main and mizzen!', he called. A few seconds was all that was needed for that very simple operation

81

(getting them in was the problem.) The vessel was now just above the Middle Hope Cove, not much more than half a cable from the rocky shore, and with the wind dead astern the strain on the helm had eased. With the current running out at about 4 to 5 knots, just at that spot the *Mary Fletcher* was only doing some two knots over the ground. Without the topsail she would never have made it to the anchorage. But only about a mile to go, and still nearly two hours to low water. Rounding the head, George edged her in out of the tide race, called to Arthur to run the topsail down and was amused to see Captain Trumper run forward to give the cook a hand. Under the lee of the hill the wind lost its force. With Clevedon Pier open just clear of Wains Hill the mate called 'Run down the jibs' and, as the sails came rasping down the stays, he put the helm down and rounded the *Mary Fletcher*'s head to wind. The captain let go the staysail halyard, George called to Arthur to let go the anchor as soon as he saw the ship was making sufficient stern way. Eighteen hours after starting to load in the Newport river the *Mary Fletcher* was quietly at anchor with her 130 tons of cargo near the mouth of the river Yeo, and during that time the crew had managed a fair night's sleep.

The captain, walking aft where George was lowering the peak of the mizzen said 'You handled her well George, very well. You saved us a tide too!' 'Done it quite a few times in the old *Sarah*', said George, 'no hope though with the wind easterly. We might be able to get her up to the pier tonight if its not overcast, there's nearly a full moon.' George noticed the captain looking to the eastward obviously trying to locate the river's mouth. But the river Yeo peters out as it flows on to the wide expanse of the mud flats and from seaward can only be picked out at highwater. Training the binoculars to where he knew the river was the mate was glad to see the 'bushy stick' was still standing where he and his father had stuck it in about five years before on the lowest part of the bar, about three quarters of a mile away. All this was pointed out to Captain Trumper, who was quick to realise that the only way a stranger could find the mouth of the Yeo from seaward would be to wait for high water when the course of the river could be seen between the saltings. A welcome call from Arthur to say dinner was ready reminded them they had not eaten, or even had a cup of tea, since they were dropping down the river Usk.

Whilst enjoying that repast, they felt the vessel tilt a little. It was now nearing low water and the *Mary Fletcher* had touched the ground. 'Nothing to worry about', George said, 'the bed of the 'gut' shifts its course in accordance with the movement of the Langford Grounds after a long spell of easterly or westerly winds. But the channel around the Head itself is always there,' he added. After dinner, and the mate had made sure the lead of the anchor chain was such that the ship, when the flood returned, would swing clear of her anchor, the crew turned into their bunks with the alarm in the cabin set for four o'clock.

Rested and refreshed, at that hour the captain and George set the mizzen whilst Arthur brewed the inevitable mugs of tea. George's plan was simple; the wind was still fresh and westerly, and he estimated there would still be enough daylight left by the time there was sufficient water over the bar, for out on the flats in twilight the muddy water of the incoming tide would be the same colour as the mud itself. Only the sapling, the 'bushy stick', would be the real guide.

With the anchor hove up just clear of the water, and the standing jib set, George took the helm and with a favourable wind and tide, the *Mary Fletcher* stood up towards the mouth of the Yeo. Although Arthur was stationed in the bows to look out for the 'bushy stick' it was the mate who, knowing where to look, saw it first. The captain, at the mate's suggestion, stood by the jib halyard ready to let it go when George gave the word, and Arthur stood by the down-haul ready to haul the sail down. That particular evening the sunset and moonrise fortunately coincided to within a few minutes. Only about a cable's length to go now. The mate had warned Captain Trumper they were a bit early, and that the vessel may well 'smell the ground' as they crossed the bar, 'but we've got no speed cap'n with this bit of sail, and if we touch its all soft mud!'

The ship was nearly abreast of the marker now. All three men felt it, just a gentle lift of the decks under their feet, and a noticeable drag in the momentum of the ship but only for a couple of moments of time. Loaded as she was, plus her own weight, she just slid over. 'Down jib!', came the call from George, and in a few seconds it was down. The river there was less than half a cable wide, and a short kink in its course thereabout made it necessary to luff the ship up nearly head to wind but only for about two of her lengths to keep her off the opposite bank. With the helm hard down and the mizzen boom hauled in by Captain Trumper, the old vessel, travelling only at a walking pace, did exactly as the mate hoped she would – forged ahead nearly head to wind, helped by the stream, and reached the next bend.

Calling to Arthur to hoist up the jib again, and asking the captain to ease off the mizzen sheet, the *Mary Fletcher* with the wind abeam was now in the stretch of river between the saltings, and it was still one and a half hours to high water. Meantime the moon, nearly full, was well above the horizon unobscured by any cloud. Captain Trumper, standing beside George said,

'That's not the first time you carried out that manoeuvre George. I would never have attempted it myself.'

George replied,

'Neither would anybody else, without they were mad, not knowing what was under their bottom. As it happens there's nothing but soft mud.'

Less than half an hour brought them up to Pugs Pit, which is a little pill where the river bends and is wider than most places. Here George called to Arthur to take down the jib and at the same time he put the helm down and stuck the ship's bows into the weather bank. The tide and the wind in the mizzen swung her stern upstream.

Came the call to Arthur to lower the anchor down to the forefoot and, as soon as she floated clear, to give her about six fathom of chain. They were now within three cables' length of the discharging berth. In a few minutes the rising tide lifted the vessel's bow clear and, as she made stern way, her bow was sheered off to the centre of the river, the anchor let go and five or six fathom of cable paid out, not to bring the ship up, but enough to keep her head to the stream whilst dragging the anchor along the river's bed acted as a drogue. In a little over half an hour they were abreast of the Weston, Clevedon and Portishead Light Railway's wharf beside the river. Leaving the anchor off in the river, the mate sheered the vessel in, whilst Arthur paid out the chain cable. The *Mary Fletcher* came to rest beside the piles with the slightest of bumps. Only now to moor her with plenty of 'drift' to the bow and stern ropes and all was well. Not being yet high water and the *Mary Fletcher* loaded deep as she was, the sea banks on either side of the river were higher than eye level to the crew on the deck. Captain Trumper looked around at the moonlit scene with wonder in his eyes.

'Don't anybody live hereabouts George?'

Pointing to the upright ladder fixed to the piles, George replied:

'If you'll go up the ladder you'll see all the lights that are here to see. All the land for miles around is below sea level by nearly ten feet.'

The nearest light the captain could see from the deck of the pier was about a quarter of a mile away. It was the window of a farmhouse. As far as the eye could see on either side were the lights of dwellings, few and far between. A blaze of lights to the north east was the town of Clevedon, and to the south west some miles away the lights of Worlebury Hill. It made him feel the spot to which he had brought the *Mary Fletcher* was the loneliest place on earth!

Arthur coming aft to George and taking advantage of the captain's absence on the pier said: 'Blimee George! No wonder you'm a wild man!! I never seed a place as dreary as this – not even in Ireland.'"

Notes on Contributors

David J Starkey is Research Fellow in the Maritime History of Devon in the Departments of History and Archaeology, and of Economic History, at the University of Exeter. His published work includes various studies of eighteenth-century British privateering enterprise.

William Ravenhill is Emeritus Reardon Smith Professor of Geography at the University of Exeter. He has published extensively on the history of British cartography, particularly its development in the Renaissance and early modern periods.

Alan Carr was formerly with the Nature Conservancy and thereafter with the Institute of Oceanographic Sciences at Taunton until its closure. He now works as a consultant. His interests are mainly in coastal geomorphology, sediment transport and conservation.

Alan Southward is Leverhulme Senior Fellow at the Marine Biological Association in Plymouth. His wide-ranging research interests include studies of long-term changes in marine life in south-west England and the Western Approaches.

Gerald Boalch is a marine botanist at the Plymouth Marine Laboratory. His publications include studies of long-term changes in the plant life of the English Channel.

Linda Maddock is a Research Fellow at the Marine Biological Association in Plymouth. She has worked on many aspects of marine biology and oceanography and is particularly interested in long-term changes.

Peter Allington is ship's keeper and master of the sailing barge *Shamrock* at the National Maritime Museum's out-station at Cotehele Quay, Cornwall. He formerly served on the sail training vessel *Halcyon* at the College of Nautical Studies, Warsash, Southampton. The holder of a Master's Certificate (Home Trade), he has worked extensively in the coastal trade.